Yours, Sincerely

Millie Blue Capon

Copyright © 2024 Millie Blue Capon

The moral right of Millie Blue Capon to be recognised as the creator of this original work has been asserted. All rights reserved. No part of this publication may be reproduced, distributed, or transmitted in any form or by any means, including photocopying, recording, or other electronic or mechanical methods, without the prior written permission of the author, except in the case of brief quotations embodied in critical reviews, and certain other non-commercial uses where permitted by local legislation.

Edited by Lora Rovegna
Layout by Oliver Tooley
Cover design by Julia Hartsoe

Published by Blue Poppy Publishing
87 High Street, Ilfracombe, Devon, EX34 9NH

ISBN: 978-1-83778-039-6
First Edition

A CIP catalogue record for this book is available from the British Library.

Table Of Contents

Introduction	1
Chapter One | Telling A Story	3
Chapter Two | Letters From Nature (Part I)	13
Chapter Three | Words of Wisdom	19
Chapter Four | Facing Uncertainty	33
Chapter Five | The Power of Love (Part I)	45
Chapter Six | To the One Who…	55
Chapter Seven | Music for the Soul	73
Chapter Eight | Open When….	87
Chapter Nine | Letters from Nature (Part II)	99
Chapter Ten | Looking Up and Looking On	113
Chapter Eleven | Written In Colour	121
Chapter Twelve | Fighting Feeling	131
Chapter Thirteen | The Power of Love (Part II)	147
Chapter Fourteen | To A Perfect Stranger	159
Chapter Fifteen | The Unwritten Letter	171
Acknowledgements	177
Who Can I Turn To?	179

Introduction

Dear reader, welcome to the first letter of *Yours, Sincerely*. I always imagined that writing an opening to a book would be straightforward (how wrong I was). For when I thought about writing this, in my head, the words flowed out without a second thought. In practice, it has proved challenging to find the words to express why writing this book has been so important to me. That being said, here we are, and I'm grateful to share this space with you.

In July 2021, I put out an online survey calling for anonymous writing prompts for a series of letters. I'll admit that I was surprised to see letter requests pouring in so quickly. As the prompts showed up in my inbox and I began writing, I couldn't help but see life in a new light. Consequently, these became letters that celebrated what it is to live life in all its messy glory! I feel honoured that strangers would welcome me to write responses to their prompts, each searching for something different. From lists of purple things to letters on insecurity and vulnerability, the prompts that I received were unique, encouraging me to creatively shape narratives around what it is to live and to love.

I want to preface *Yours, Sincerely* by stating that these letters come in all shapes and sizes. They honour both rawness and reality, acknowledging that life can be both painful and beautiful, while still making space for frivolity and childhood anecdotes to make you smile. Ultimately, these 100 letters are written between all of us; I just happen to have had the privilege of narrating them.

Like all of us, my story has known peaks and valleys, moments where I have felt love and light, but also moments where I have felt distant from both. However, through it all, I've always been in search of hope, and that is why *Yours, Sincerely* became a book. My book.

I hope that these letters are representative of our stories, embracing those parts of ourselves that we often keep hidden while celebrating the joy that living can bring us. While I acknowledge that some circumstances can't be changed by the words I have written, I was keen to write a book that brought hope into seemingly hopeless situations – something that I know I would have found useful through some of the valleys I have experienced.

As you read this, I am reaching out to you with all the love in the world. For all the challenges that come your way, I hope an equal amount of lightness finds its way to you. Life's complexities may leave you uncertain of many things but know that your worthiness of love does not change with the seasons; it remains a constant that you can be sure of.

It is a special feeling to know that one day somebody will be sitting, holding this book that I have written, and reading not only my story but experiencing the stories of others. I dared not believe that I'd be here to see this, but I am – and it's everything and more!

Yours Sincerely,
Millie Blue Capon x

Chapter One | Telling A Story

The Letter's Journey

(inspired by the prompt
'a letter about a letter')

A letter's journey begins at the first thought of writing. You imagine the recipient and where they might be, before turning your attention to the page.

You follow this up by letting the words spill out – formal prose, poetic verse, or on the brim of overflowing with something on your heart. The letter holds our innermost thoughts, shouldering the weight of our feelings. It takes on the responsibility of ensuring that nothing gets lost in translation – bridging the gap between family, friends, and strangers.

Once the words settle upon the page, the paper is folded and pushed into an envelope that securely holds the letter. The letter is then posted, transported, sorted through, and delivered – taking a rather exciting adventure between countries, cities, towns, and villages – from the hands of one to another.

When it reaches its destination, it is pushed through the letterbox, the metal clinking once the letter has dropped to the floor. It lies in wait for the recipient claiming it – when it can begin to create its impact.

Letters have evolved in content and delivery, but even now, we delight ourselves in the traditional values of letters. A letter can be anything you'd like it to be; it's like the umbrella term for any sort of written note. I like a letter that leaves an impression. So, as I write these letters, I fill them with traditional sentiments, leaving space for modern love letters to form.

The writer in me wants to encourage you to leave your mark on a blank page and watch the journey unfold – you never know where *one* letter might lead you next.

This Is My Why

(inspired by the prompt
'how to tell a story')

Storytelling is an innate part of the human experience. From conversations about the here and now to exploring stories from our past, storytelling is a significant part of connecting with others and forming relationships.

Within day-to-day exchanges, and in broader discussions of our biggest dreams and greatest fears, there is so much depth to the experience of telling our stories. Our stories carry the weight of the experiences that we have had, the places that we'd like to go to, and the overall essence of who we are. When we share our stories, we open ourselves up to exploring the ups and downs of life itself while holding a place for those parts of us that we keep beneath the surface. It is therefore not surprising that when we come to tell these stories, the question of how we tell them is one that stopped me in my tracks.

The letters in this book are all stories, and they began to be written long before any ink hit the page; they came alive when I understood that someone somewhere might need to hear these words. The 'how' became clearer as I established *why* it was that I wanted to write between the lines of the stories of strangers and connect individuals in this way. 'How' has been different with each story, suggesting that there is no right way to tell a story.

Allowing space for your story to *exist* is still a valid form of telling your story. Your story matters even in the unspoken words. Telling your story, in one form or another, could be about coming to a place of inner peace or providing yourself with an opportunity to embrace those feelings that haven't yet had space to be felt. Your story is worthy of taking its place wherever, and however, it needs to.

The Little Things

(inspired by the prompt 'a memory that makes you smile')

Each individual is a cumulation of things that they've experienced and the innate parts of who they are. Sharing our experiences can be an opportunity to meet each other with empathy and share in the seemingly insignificant moments of one another's lives. Moments of shared experience are the memories, for me, that last a lifetime. My favourite memories are often those that I share with others that can be told from multiple points of view. I love conversational exchanges of 'Do you remember when?' before the discussion flows into the trading of memories. There is a sense of unity in these conversations, even when we experience life differently.

This letter called for 'A Memory That Made Me Smile', but the truth is that there are so many to choose from. This prompt has brought fragments of memories to the forefront that I would not have ever considered. You might not realise it but even writing this letter is a moment in time I wish I could fully capture with words. How beautiful it is to have the opportunity of writing to you while my head overflows with memories.

I love hearing other people talk about their memories, and I live for the tiny details that build the picture of what another person has experienced. My friend Jack is one of the best storytellers I know. They will turn to me and say, 'You'll never guess what' before giving an animated account of something that has happened. I love the nuanced details Jack sprinkles throughout – they somehow enhance the experience of hearing the story – making the whole thing an immersive experience.

With a breadth of memories making themselves known to me now, I felt it would be a pity to restrict myself to just one memory that has made me smile. While this letter recounts moments I treasure, I sincerely hope some of your memorable moments bridge the gap between us.

First breath, morning light,
  forty winks, a chapter at bedtime.
Sunrise, elevenses, evening supper,
  and the seasonal setting of the sun.

A child's pottery wheel, patchwork blankets,
  a wooden dollhouse, a stripey mouse.
Car picnics, study breaks, city walks,
  and muddy wellington boots.

PJ days, pizza bagels,
  the fresh air calm before the storm.
Highclere Castle, beach walks with rainbows,
  deep breath; lungs filled to the overflow.

Bonfires in winter, driving during spring,
  summer reading, autumnal walks.
Jack Frost, April showers, White Horses,
  and October's array of cosy TV.

Patience for trying seasons,
  joy in the little things.
Learning to be bold, having time to reflect,
  connecting and taking my place.

A first concert, first date,
  first kiss, peace prevails.
Lasting loves, final farewells,
  and seemingly insignificant moments to cherish.

The Joy of Escapism

(inspired by, and featuring, a creative narrative prompt)

My family would be the first to tell you that as a youngster I had a wild imagination. This was particularly evident in the anecdotes I would tell them. For example, when amongst the waves of assorted British beaches, or when exploring the shallows of the rock pools, my stories would include sightings of every creature imaginable. As I would proclaim my sightings with excitement, and as my siblings followed in my footsteps, my fictional tales became associated with the lovingly named 'Millie's Magic Goggles'. I found so much joy in sharing these moments with my family, and much to my delight, they humoured my enthusiasm.

Escaping into a world of storytelling can be freeing. For years, I have found liberation in escapism and pleasure in sharing my stories with those around me – particularly as a child. Nowadays, my stories appear to be rooted in realism, but perhaps this letter might inspire me to return to fictional tales. Only now am I appreciating the contentment it brought me to imagine beyond what I could see. These fabricated underwater scenes fed my soul in ways I couldn't consciously realise as a child, but now I can remember, cherish, and embrace them.

Dear reader, may you never lose the childlike joy found in escapism. I hope that you can allow yourself to dream and imagine. In this moment, let go of the chaos around you and escape with me…

In my own world, I watch out for what lies beneath the surface of the water. The sun, warm on my back, glistens in the pools between the rocks as it illuminates the creatures that make their home here. Peering in, hand cupping my forehead and resting on my temple, I can see the water alive with sea life.

From tiny shrimp to blennies darting between strawberry anemones, there is an underwater kingdom to get lost in; a realm we explore curiously yet have a limited understanding of its capacity.

To the left, I see a starfish, pink tentacles stretched out as though preparing to give a giant hug. They linger on the sidelines but make themselves seen with their bold colours, wide embrace, and understated beauty. I am in awe of their subtle stance – no hesitation in taking up space, although finding satisfaction in the place that feels right for them. My eyes follow the hermit crabs as they scuttle in the shallows – youthful energy in abundance. Shell in tow, they move seamlessly across the sand, almost bounding across the rock pool floor.

I wander until my feet meet the shallows of the sea. The water playfully splashes at my ankles, refreshing as the sun continues to shine. The rock pools funnel me to the open waters; the ocean calling me, inviting me to go deeper. Limpets litter the rocks, clinging tightly as the waves ride up to them. I let my mind wander; the reflection of the clouds in the water disturbing my view of the water's inhabitants. Dolphins dance in the afternoon sunlight; seals bask at the edge of the shore. They find peace in the stillness while embracing the water's movements.

Eyes wide and heart open, I catch a glimpse of mermaids, their garden guarded by an enchanting sleeping green sea dragon. Charmed by the mystery that lies in the underwater kingdom, I find a sense of belonging here – magic goggles enabling me to see beyond what is really here so that I might immerse myself fully in the great unknown.

Light and Shadows

(inspired by the prompt 'telling your story')

Though our experiences in life are different, we share our stories as a way of relating to one another. Telling your own story can be a daunting experience. We can feel exposed when we try to articulate the way we feel and the things that we have experienced, and it can be challenging to find the words to explain the places that we have been. If and/or when you tell your story, know that you can reveal joy and pain – the light and the shadow parts of you.

There can be relief in being seen for the first time, though it can also be overwhelming. Sometimes we might feel such a deep sense of shame that we can't own our stories just yet, and that is okay too (though there is no shame in where you have been). How you share your story and live out your truth is up to you. There is no pressure to tell people how you came to the point you are at now; you don't owe your story to anybody. Sharing parts of *my* story has strengthened me in some ways, but in others, the day-to-day living out of my truth feels just as powerful. Each breath you take is proof that you are here and your story matters.

I hope you find the strength to own your story and that you see where the light can glow through. You might share your story by honouring the strength that whispers 'tomorrow I will try again', or maybe you will open up in quiet conversations. Perhaps your voice will crack, or the tears may fall silently, but I hope the burden that you carry lightens.

The words may get jumbled or flow in gentle verse. They might be in a secret journal, or you may find a platform to say the words clearly and confidently without reservation. Your story matters regardless of how you share it, even in the things that you wish had happened differently.

Chapter Two | Letters From Nature
(Part I)

Grow Through What You Go Through

(inspired by the prompt
'grow through what you go through')

Over time, I have come to believe that not all experiences require a life lesson. However, I do believe that it is possible to find places where the light can glow through the things that we go through. It is therefore possible to grow in *light* of our circumstances, as opposed to because of them, and come out stronger on the other side. I've never taken to the phrase 'everything happens for a reason'. I worry that we use this proverb in place of anything better to say. In writing this letter, I offer an alternative perspective; some words of encouragement that honour the complexity of our experiences and the natural process of growth.

Let me ask you this: do you shame sunflowers in their slower seasons, or do you praise them for their strength in a day-to-day search for the sun and allow their yellow petals to unfold one at a time? So then why do we expect so much instantaneously from ourselves? When did we decide that we must pace ourselves faster than the natural course of nature around us? Dear reader, it may feel like you are buried deep but, like a sunflower, seek the light and grow towards it. Even in seasons of gradual growth, it is beautiful to see you flourish.

Growth may take time, and sometimes it can *feel* like we will never come through to the light. Be kind to yourself in this season of waiting. There may not be a purpose to your pain, but there is a purpose in you! When our lives are fuelled by remaining present and seeing the beauty in the smallest of growths, we may just find a greater sense of peace in it all.

Have patience and free yourself from the expectation that change has to happen quickly. I promise you that the light is there when you are ready to seek it out. You will flourish in time and your circumstances will not keep you in the darkness forever.

The Long Stretch Home

(inspired by the prompt
'roots')

When the sun sinks beneath the tips of the pines, the old souls awaken as day turns to night. They sigh, breathing in and allowing their lungs to expand fully before exhaling. With each breath that the trees take, their roots deepen with subtle movements, inching towards a better-grounded state. Those roots hold the pine's secrets and stories while entwining with the roots from neighbouring trees. There is strength in their perseverance, beauty in their gnarly growth, and a presence of a woven community.

Slow down,
the stability that you long for
is within the earth in which you grow.

Sad Duck Days

(inspired by the prompt 'ducks')

Have you ever found yourself experiencing a sad duck day, where even the lightest shower of rain feels like a downpour? Nothing, in particular, has happened, but the world weighs heavily on you, and the sadness sneaks its way in. The kind of day where you long to be seen while simultaneously wanting to hide away. An old secondary school teacher of mine once described this as a sad duck day, and it has stuck with me ever since.

For some, the heaviness is momentary, whereas, for others, the sad duck days seem to arrive one after the other (neither being better or worse). When a sad duck day is upon you, I hope the storm lifts to a drizzle, even if it's fleeting. With time, you'll find what you need to keep the rain at bay, or you'll learn to dance within it as the ducks do. Their webbed feet create ripples – forming a rhythm with a steadiness that carries them through even the rainiest of days.

Make a Splash

(inspired by the prompt
'a letter from the rain')

One afternoon during a week of perfect summer, the rain came. The droplets appeared slowly at first, trickling down the window and misting up my view of the city from my flat window. However, the gentle pitter-patter picked up pace, and before I knew it, they cascaded from the sky, falling ferociously. They merged, the wind forcing them together so that they chaotically strode down the glass. *That's it*, I thought, *I can't go out now* – but I did.

I made my way to the park in a midi skirt and black T-shirt. The water appeared as speckled gems on the surface of my skin, dripping down my face (smudging the eyeliner, of course). The wind whispered through Everton Park carrying the sweet smell of rainfall. The afternoon sunlight danced over the ground, reflecting off the pavement. With my black boots laced up tightly, my feet darted between the puddles. After a quick look around, I ran to the final puddle at the end of the path and laughed quietly to myself as I jumped into joy wholeheartedly.

It didn't matter that the rain hadn't stopped, although I enjoyed watching the blue sky appear from the brow of the park. The rain came, and I found joy anyway.

To the one who reads this letter, let the rain come – embrace it even! Allow the rain space to be as it needs to be and to do as it needs to do. Then, go out there and make a splash. Choose to absorb existing in all its fullness in any way that moves you.

Someone once said to me, 'If you can feel it, then it is purpose-filled'. For all the dampness and drizzle, there is an equal amount of delight to be found in it. On the inside looking out, it appears sombre, saddening even, but from within it, it is enchanting – an invitation to seek out the renewal of childlike joy.

Chapter Three | Words of Wisdom

Passion Centred

(inspired by the prompt 'building a career on passion')

The things that you are passionate about are no accident. Passion is where a spirit or dream materialises into something with an ambitious drive. It is more than just enthusiasm; passion is a compelling emotion that *leads* to motive. While we may be driven by purpose, dreams are sustained with passion. To be passion centred is to allow your life to be *shaped* by such desire. I was fortunate that my parents encouraged me to live passionately, so here are a few things to remember when considering the role of passion in *your* life…

1. You are free to pursue passion; you can find and explore new passions, and you can be a person with many passions. The main challenge you'll face is allowing them into fruition.
2. Passion thrives when we allow our motives to shift to a place where we are not relying on someone else's validation or approval.
3. It is possible to find passion in the process and imperfections. I'm not sure when the world started telling us that we needed to be good at everything that we do, but at some point, we made passion about achievement. Be experimental and enjoy trying new things!
4. When passion sits at your core, doors will open for you that you never expected. Write that book, make that music, bake that cake, and run your race. Passion shifts your mindset from what, how, and when to why – and that in itself can be an exciting thing.
5. Life is too short to not be all in. Only now am I coming to see the value in fully embracing the things that I am most passionate about. Commit wholeheartedly to your passions, and your life will change in ways you are yet to imagine.

Self-Security

(inspired by the prompt 'insecurity')

Trust me, we have all experienced insecurity, no matter how self-assured a person might seem. It's that niggly little voice that whispers 'You're not quite good enough'; I find that it shows up at the most inconvenient times. The fact is that insecurity is something to acknowledge and work through.

It might be hard to imagine that I have had to confront my own insecurities to bring these letters into being. It has been challenging to believe that my words could earn the right to be written. I have faced doubts over whether I am qualified enough to write this book or secure enough in myself to offer something of value. In expressing that I am a work in progress, I can bring this letter to you without holding back.

Before choosing to make peace with the most unique parts of myself, I felt overlooked and judged (by those closest to me and even by those who didn't know me). In one of my lowest seasons, I couldn't hear anything positive that was said to me or about me. Lines blurred and even words spoken with the purest intentions got lost in translation. I was innately insecure, and the voices became louder than niggles. As I learn to make peace with myself and move towards self-love, I can start to see myself the way that others do – the *reality* instead of my perceived reality.

You too *deserve* to live peacefully with yourself. I wish I had embraced this truth much sooner than I did. Even now, I wish that I dared to live this out as I encourage you to do. While the road to self-love is anything but linear, I would encourage you to affirm yourself gently – aim for neutrality if that feels more attainable. Compassionately allow the truth to be your foundation so that you can live within the self-security that I know you deserve.

The Boat in the Harbour

(inspired by the prompt 'anchors')

A veteran of the brine and an old timer of the sea – a knackered rowing boat arrives in the harbour where an anchor is thrown overboard. They'll wait a while in the harbour until it is safe to sail once more. The boat finds rest, and before long they are at one with the waves around them. When the time is right, the anchor will be lifted, and they'll be on their way again.

From doing a little research, I discovered that an anchor is defined as a 'device' (something that is made, something fit for purpose). Anchors bring about calm and stability, and physically, they provide a firm foundation. They can be temporary or permanent, there are different types, and they each fulfil a unique role.

In my experience, it is important to have people around who can *anchor* you in each season. I deeply value those who remain steadfast in my life at every sign of uncertainty and those who seek to find the signs of security that I latch on to when the current stirs up trouble for my vessel. Some people anchor me in my wins when the wind picks up in my sails, but they also keep things steady when the waves are looking stormy.

Sometimes, the anchor may appear to be different; the anchor itself might not look like a person at all. The anchor could be a value or a passion that grounds and centres you when uncertainty comes your way. I find that I often rely on hope, which has a different capability to bring about stability than people can. Choosing hope is choosing something that is grounded and secure. My anchor holds steady in the turbulent waters and prepares me with what I need when I set sail again. Hope may not stop waves from beating against the boat, but it can enable the boat to hold on and move forward once the uncertainty settles.

It Takes a Village

(inspired by the prompt
'the people around you will change')

It is inevitable that as seasons come and go, new chapters in your life will bring about a change in the people that surround you; this is something that I have experienced often.

I thought I would share with you some reminders on relationships (admittedly writing as someone who could benefit from reading this letter from time to time).

1. It is okay that people come and go from your life. I used to take it personally when the people around me changed, but it is important to remember that these changes are natural.
2. Be patient with people but don't be robbed of your peace. You can be kind, loving, and gracious and still maintain boundaries that honour your feelings.
3. You can't change other people, and it is not your job to. However, you can choose to love others unconditionally, even when making this choice feels challenging. Love transcends time and distance, so even while there is space between you and another, there is capacity for love.
4. Embrace the relationships that currently surround you and allow yourself to embrace the changes when they come; goodness can come from change.
5. Refusing to let others in won't prevent you from getting hurt. I have tried the 'isolate for protection' approach, disguising it behind the mask of boundaries – it wasn't successful. We were always meant to form relationships with one another, so remind yourself that it is okay to trust people. Love can (and will) outweigh anything else that attempts to take residence.
6. There can be so much beauty in the changing relationships that we find ourselves in, though I hope that there will a constant few who will consistently show up for you.

In Perspective

(inspired by the prompt
'a letter on perspective, I'm overwhelmed by life')

Overwhelm, to some extent, is a survival strategy; it is the point where we begin to acknowledge all that is around us. Overwhelm changes our vision, forcing our bodies to respond (not always to our detriment). The risk of overwhelm is that we see life with tunnel vision while simultaneously taking in everything from our peripherals to prove the need for overwhelm. Overwhelm can distort the ability to see clearly because no matter how much we try to take things one moment at a time, we are bearing the weight of too much to the point where we may not respond as we would in a clear state of being. In all honesty, I haven't quite worked out how to navigate overwhelm myself, but I am learning that perspective can make a difference in how overwhelm feels for me.

Overwhelm makes it possible to forget that you are part of something bigger; you might believe it all comes down to you or that you are the cause of your overwhelm. However, picture a tree for a moment – a tree filled with tones of orange in the height of autumn. A leaf on a tree when surrounded by thousands of others feels okay. When the leaf tumbles, it would be easy to feel out of control, even if it is held and carried by the wind amongst hundreds of others. Eventually, the leaf lands and looks back at where it has fallen from and can note that the seasons have simply changed. It was never about the leaf itself. Perspective works best when we allow our peripheral vision to rationalise our thoughts rather than heighten our overwhelm.

I hear you when you say that everything feels bigger than you are right now. This restless uncertainty will not last forever. For every moment that life feels like an insurmountable challenge, hold close to the truth that you are going to be okay. You do not have to have all the answers figured out to be able to find peace in not knowing.

A Thought on Sensitivity

(inspired by the prompt
'am I too sensitive?')

Sensitivity is a complex quality. While I have learned to believe that sensitivity is a quality that paves the way for the essence of who I am, learning to appreciate it has not been straightforward. My understanding of this attribute is that it is a capacity within each of us that allows us to respond to what surrounds us. Every one of us has sensitivity, a unique way of taking in the world and reacting to it, but some of us are inevitably more sensitive than others. 'Too sensitive' is a phrase that surrounds many of us, making it hard to embrace sensitivity as a strength – but there is so much more to sensitivity than meets the eye. The sensitivity that might present challenges is the same sensitivity that comes into its own when needed most…

Perhaps we need to reframe how much we gain from the sensitivity within us. Sensitivity allows us to feel the feelings of others and affords us the ability to build relationships with sincerity. Those who are sensitive connect and respond with intuition in ways that others can't. Sensitivity facilitates an ability to be creative. Sensitivity is a profound intuition. There is nothing innately wrong with being sensitive, so how is it possible to be *too* sensitive? You're not too much, you're just enough. Harnessing sensitivity so that it is our strength is a journey. There is beauty in self-exploration, and there is no need to compress or resent your sensitivity for the benefit of others. Let it glow out of you so that the strength of your sensitivity is irrefutable. May you know that every part of you is welcome here.

Never too much, just enough as you are. Connect with that sensitive part of you – cherish it and be proud of the wonderful way that it syncs you with the world. Sensitivity is a beautiful quality that few embrace, so claim it as yours and be curious about its potential.

Wild and Free

(inspired by the prompt 'the inner child')

Inner Child, you chase after adventure with every fibre of your being – without being afraid of the uncertainty. Eyes wild, heart light and expectant, you throw your arms out and embrace all that lies ahead of you. There is so much to be gained from embracing the childlike joy you bring. At some point, you might feel squashed or forgotten altogether, but don't allow the shame of what has been, or your fear of what is to come, to stop you from catching moments in time with both hands. You make us whole – don't forget how important you are.

The world tends to dampen the sense of adventure that our inner child is so keen to pursue. With time, our zest for life can fizzle out, leaving us distant from our inner child. *My* advice would be to free yourself from whatever it is that keeps you from living curiously. If your inner child is anything like mine, generally, it's the little things that excite you and build that sense of living freely. From blowing bubbles to watching the seeds fly off a dandelion clock, there are infinite tiny ways to excite the child within you.

Regardless of what has come before and what lies ahead, embrace your inner child wholeheartedly. Your inner child will make the ordinary extraordinary, make the hours feel like minutes, and see you through life's valleys until you find your way again. Take hold of adventure with both hands and don't allow the weight of the burdens you carry to hold you back from finding possibility in the everyday.

At the core of yourself, you will find everything you could ever need for it is already within you. Choose to love yourself completely and embrace whatever it is that holds you back. Rediscover the dreams, schemes, and longings to be and chase all those childhood destinies that you once dreamed of so clearly.

A Letter from Frankie

(inspired by the prompt
'a letter for someone learning to drive')

Learning to drive is an experience that goes beyond the moment that you pass your test. Despite some low-level anxiety, I was fortunate to pass the first time and to take to the road with relative ease. However, it is true what they say – you don't learn to drive until you're out there on your own but, the truth is, I have never truly been alone. I am one of those people who names their car. Frankie, a little red Toyota Yaris, my first car, taught me everything I would ever need to know about driving. She guided me through exhilarating joys, and she was present through many lows too. It sounds daft, but if you've been there, then you know how much a car can come to mean to you. If you've yet to experience the joy, or you have made the valid choice not to learn to drive, then I hope you will enjoy a little road trip through some of the lessons that Frankie taught me, about driving and about life.

The Joy in the Unexpected

Frankie took her place on the driveway before I had even passed my test. After doing a week's intensive driving course, I was set on passing, though I was doubtful that I could manage it the first time. My parents were away on holiday, and I booked my test with just a few days' notice. After hatching a plan with my gran (the only other person who knew about the test), I was good to go.

Aside from a last-minute panic about the whereabouts of my windscreen wipers as the rain began to pour during my test, I, to our surprise, passed with flying colours – and a few tears! Telling my gran was easily one of the most joyous things I've ever experienced, and Frankie bore witness to it from the comfort of our driveway. Somehow, the unexpected joys in life are laced with a little magic.

Passing my test left me on cloud nine, and I was excited to share more moments like this with Frankie. Early lessons from Frankie were to allow joy in, embrace the magic in the unexpected, and remember you'll always discover the windscreen wipers in the storms – even if it is a bit of a scramble.

Finding My Way

One of the first purchases I made once I'd passed my driving test was a satellite navigation system. Just days after passing, I made the journey to Devon to visit family – a two-hour expedition south on the dreaded motorway and across the country lanes. The satnav was next to useless, repetitively telling me to 'make a U-turn where possible' so I followed my dad's lead and ignored it. I wouldn't recommend heading North if you're trying to make your way south.

As nerve-wracking as it was, I have lived to tell the tale. As time passed, I have learned to embrace the unplanned routes and the surprises along the way, which is lucky really. With each route and reroute, the wheels have taken me on one heck of a journey, and, for the most part, I've loved every second. The second bit of advice that Frankie gave me was to trust the process of following my nose, for I will always find my way.

Sharing Time, Sharing Space, Sharing Love

One experience of driving I was most looking forward to was being able to road trip with the music loud and windows down. Singing in the car founded many of my friendships and family relationships from early on in my life – so much so that hosting this sacred space was an experience I longed for.

Jack taught me that singing to millennial hits and show tunes alongside your pals is one of life's simplest joys – the rest of the world fades away, and any signs or feelings of isolation appear to vanish too.

Emma was the first victim (sorry, guest) to become a passenger in my car. Em would vouch that I have become an increasingly confident driver, and I now fully relish in the joy of the stereo being turned up to top volume. Watching close friends and family fall in love with Frankie enabled me to fall in love with driving. So, the third lesson that Frankie demonstrated to me was that sharing time and space with those you love in the simplest of ways is entirely magical; tandem experiences make everything brighter.

Holding Out for a Tow Truck

Frankie taught me about the art of patience – a lesson I didn't expect to learn from driving. I never imagined feeling limited by Frankie – after all, I had learned to find my way across the hills and valleys and had grown so much as an individual. That being said, it's like Frankie knew that there were still valuable lessons to learn from our adventures together. The penultimate bit of advice that Frankie gifted to me is that just at the moment you feel furthest from a resolution, you become one step closer to one – with each minute that passes, the rescue team draws closer to dropping off a petrol can for the final stretch of the dual carriageway, or the tow truck lights glow behind you as they agree to tow your written off car home.

Goodbye Little Red Car

Goodbyes are tough, even if you're just waving off your first car. By the time I had to see her towed away from our driveway, Frankie wasn't just a car; she was my safe place, and she'd come to be a representation of so many accumulated memories. While learning to drive, you never anticipate getting attached to the delicate shell that takes you from A to B, but I am glad that I allowed her to be more than just a car to me, even if that made it harder to say goodbye. Frankie will forever be my favourite car. Learning to drive was also about learning to live in a whole new way – a gift that will, without a doubt, continue to shape my life.

The Pursuit of Wholeness

(inspired by the prompts:
how do I 'discover who I am?' and 'create myself')

Identity is something that many people wrestle with, but what do we do when it feels as if we have forgotten to appreciate the essence of who we are? I wish that there was a simple answer.

Trust me, although I can't pretend to know the ins and outs of the experiences within each story of those reading this letter, I know that the search for peace within our identity can be challenging. What I do know is that though each experience of identity is different, our uniqueness was not a mistake.

Therefore, I hope you choose to lay down the burden of uncovering who you are and choose, instead, to welcome curiosity. For those moments where your questions of identity seem to rock your world, I have put together these reminders that I hope will speak to where you are.

- When self-love feels like a far-off reality, perhaps it's okay to acknowledge that who you are has brought you to this point. Each new day presents us with the opportunity to continue establishing our story, graciously and unapologetically.
- It appears to take a bold audacity to live authentically – allowing ourselves into the spotlight opens us up to a world of scrutiny from all angles. However, life is too short to waste time void of peace in who we are. Step into your greatness, wherever you believe it to be, and know that I am rooting for you on this journey (encourage each other too). While self-discovery can overwhelm you, trust that freedom can be found in uncovering who you are.
- Your story does not get to be defined or gatekept by somebody else. You do not owe anyone an explanation, and you're free to define and redefine yourself beyond binaries.

- There are beautiful moments of artistry that come into play when we consider identity, but the very core of you is whole from day one and remains so. We gather pieces of ourselves along the way, at times facing unjust challenges, but remember that your essence is the part of you that remains consistently wonderful from the beginning.

Sometimes I think about how our lives are like a patchwork blanket. I imagine you might be picturing something seamlessly soft, but the one that I see is a little different. I see a patchwork creation, crafted with intricacy, the pieces held together with strength, love, and purpose. The patches feel as though they shouldn't fit together, but somehow, they are arranged as something rather beautiful. I imagine life to be like that – messy but tenaciously formed, flawed in many ways – though the story behind it allows us to see that it is crafted to perfection.

Each part of our lives and ourselves forms pieces of the blanket. Along the way, we gather pieces of tapestry and find a way of piecing them together. From the essence of who we are to the experiences we have and the love that weaves it all together, the patchwork blanket of our lives is unique and complex, something to be marvelled at, even in the process.

When I think about the patchwork blanket that I am creating, sensitivity and empathy form patches while cherished friendships form others. From my work and passions to family and identity, each patch is delicate and fulfilling in different ways. Some blanket squares might represent moments in my life that haven't been so perfect. Within the process of 'creating myself', these experiences wouldn't necessarily have been what I'd have chosen, but I have woven them amongst my blanket, nevertheless. No single part of the story defines me; each one finds a way to exist alongside the others. Perfectly imperfect, the patchwork blanket of my life is complexly crafted, yet I remain whole, and my story only flourishes. Between where you are and where you'd like to be, there are moments to embrace. May you feel free to delight yourself in the wholeness of life's tapestry.

Chapter Four | Facing Uncertainty

Assurance in What We Cannot See

(inspired by the prompt 'having faith')

Given that uncertainty can disrupt any of our best-laid plans, we engage in acts of faith daily. Faith is the act or mindset of believing that things can be better than they are without the empirical evidence that says they will be. Consequently, some might say that faith encourages denial. Commonplace phrases like 'too blessed to be stressed' have a habit of denying the presence of anxiety entirely. However, I believe that to be faith-filled, we must first accept the inevitability of uncertainty – an uncomfortable prospect for many, I'm sure.

To me, having faith is acknowledging the uncertainty while still having belief in what is to come. It's an assurance in what we cannot see, an audacious courage to believe that something good can still flourish. That being said, I know at times it is easier said than done. Therefore, space also needs to be made for gentleness – for what good would faith be if it was a pressure rather than a kindness? It can be challenging to find such faith in a time of need, which is why I want to take this moment to speak with you about faith.

I'd encourage you to keep your heart open to possibility; view each day as a canvas upon which you continue to paint. You add to the painting little by little, throwing lightness in amongst the shade – accepting the uncertainty while remaining faith-filled. Somehow, I find that there is comfort in knowing that worry is a common experience – just as it is reassuring that, between us, there is enough faith to muddle through. You may not know exactly what is next for you, but I am rooting for you.

I cannot say exactly what lies ahead, but I can tell you that despite the uncertainty, you are deserving of peace. Surround yourself with people who have faith in you and will hold you through challenging seasons. Even when you lack faith in yourself, I have faith in you – an assurance for what is yet to be seen.

Finding Freedom from Comparison

(inspired by the prompt
'for the student off to university')

Despite the inevitable initial nerves, I remember being excited to start university. For the longest time, I had been dreaming of what my university experience would look like, drawing inspiration from 2000's chick flicks and Australian soaps – my Pinterest board growing alongside my anticipation for a fresh start. As September came around, I said many a 'see you soon' while packing my life into boxes. From afar, through an online lens, I watched proud parents move their children into halls, and I examined my friends' pages as they entered freshers' week and university life. Everyone appeared to be having the time of their lives. By the time I moved into halls just weeks later, my perception of how university should look was wrapped up in a warped view of perfection. Dear reader, whether off to university or looking for a word or two about finding freedom from comparison – listen up!

The beauty of the human experience is that it is unique. We each have a matchless view of the world around us, and that can be a wonderful thing. While there are experiences that we can share, it is also okay to find your way through life in a different way. When we compare in a way that is detrimental to the idea of a unique experience, we find ourselves confined by comparison – robbing us of the joy of finding our way.

Be inspired, yes, but try not to drown out the curiosity that will grant you the ability to pave *your* way. While looking around you may stir up the sense that you should be somewhere else, you're exactly where you need to be right now. Your path is your own, and you can grow here just as exquisitely. Comparison will steal peace from you, but accepting that you have chosen what is right for you and shrugging off the expectation of what you should be doing or being will allow you to flourish in ways you're yet to dream up on a Pinterest board.

Making the Bold Moves

(inspired by the prompt 'a letter on how to be spontaneous')

My relationship with spontaneity is changeable. In some ways, I approach life intrepidly, but other parts of me remain cautious. As a result of this, I think it is safe to say that examples of spontaneity in my life would appear to be inconsequential in contrast to the boldness of others. That being said, does that make me any less spontaneous than those around me?

So many throughout the pandemic season made spontaneous career changes, defining alterations to family dynamics and impulsive decisions that may impact their lives forever. I admire the defining actions that take people in alternative directions. I commend the ability to step willingly into the unknown. At times, I long for their gallantry, though I have come to accept that perhaps my small spontaneous acts are just as valid. For me, spontaneity has been more evident in day-to-day decision-making. Just recently, I paused for a moment on the way to work. As someone who likes to be early for everything, I wouldn't usually do this! I pulled over to the side of the beaten track to soak up the view of the most beautiful Devon sunrise. Birdsong echoed beyond the space, and the warmth from the sun radiated through me. I may have only stopped for a moment or two, but the experience was precious – and spontaneous in its own right. I was keen to embrace peace at a moment when my world continued to feel wildly uncertain. Seizing the seemingly mundane parts of life can be equally as bold as what we would usually associate with the art of being spontaneous.

May spontaneity be something that invigorates you, and may your boldness be rewarded by experiences that shape your world for the better. You deserve to delight in the uncharted territories of each day that dawns, even in seemingly insignificant ways. You might find that you see the world anew, refreshed with a perspective that says, 'I can do anything'.

In the Midst of Chronic Illness

(inspired by the prompt
'chronic illness')

Chronic illness is multifaceted in many ways, deeply consuming and yet, at times, unnoticeable on the surface. Close friends of mine have struggled through some of their hardest days (sometimes silently) to find themselves on the other side of a new normal, while others find themselves in a time of uncertainty, unsure of what 'normal' might look like.

I am aware (and I am glad) that chronic illness is not something that everyone will have an awareness of. In light of this, I want to take a moment to share a broader picture with you. To me, being amid chronic illness is like trying to balance an un-balanceable equation. It is waking up each day with a set of symptoms that you must somehow level out with little certainty of exactly what might come along and upset the balance. It is blindly fighting your way through the fog, living a life of fewer guarantees than most, second-guessing, overexplaining, and battling against yourself in ways that aren't entirely visible. Dear reader, if this resonates with your experience of chronic illness, know that every ounce of me longs for you to know the warmth of love, the comfort of security, and the bold presence of hope here in this moment. If this isn't your story, perhaps take a moment to listen in.

For those who know what it is like, perhaps it is somewhat comforting to know that if I could take this from you, I would. I know that I can't, and I'm not naïve in thinking that saying this will magically make you feel better. That being said, I'm here, and I'm holding space for you. Whether diagnosed, suspected, or symptomatically appreciating what it is to chronically live with this condition, may you know that your experiences are welcome here. This is not a gatekept space, nor is it a place of judgement or rejection. (There is enough medical gaslighting as it is.)

This letter simply aims to illuminate the experience of living with chronic illness and bring a little comfort to those in the midst of it.

Don't give up on yourself! Life looks different right now, much different from how you'd planned, but your worthiness remains the same. While your day-to-day looks dissimilar to anything that you've known before, I cannot reiterate enough how precious and worthy you are. People around you may come and go, but you can withstand more than you imagine.

No matter what you believe to be true, there is no shame or blame for how this season of your life came about. For a long time, I believed that there was something inherently wrong with me while convincing myself that I must have done something to deserve to be in such pain. It is a daily battle to tell myself otherwise, that there was nothing I could have done to cause or prevent this, and therefore, there is no shame in it. The same can be said of you.

My friend, you are free to feel peace in a season of in-betweens, unknowns, and possibility. Somewhere along the way, I managed to convince myself that I was a burden to others because of the endless torrent of uncertainty that surrounded my health. While my brain did a pretty good job of convincing me of this as truth, it couldn't have been further from it. I think I now better appreciate that who I am is so much more than the symptoms that at times govern my life (though I can't always tangibly feel it). So much can be true of you at one given time, and you are more than the burden that you feel you might have become.

Loved –
you are loved.
Yesterday, today, the same forever –
loved beyond all measure.

When the World Feels Unpredictable

(inspired by the prompt 'struggling with financial debt')

Hey there, I hear that things right now are difficult, more than difficult; they feel impossible. In these moments where our circumstances lack clarity, I imagine that it might feel like no one could possibly understand or make you feel like it will be okay. However, I want to extend this letter to you.

If nothing else reaches through, please hear this: whatever unpredictability you are facing, it is not bigger than you, even when it feels like it is. Life is inherently unpredictable. Regardless of how much we try to plan or manoeuvre the chess pieces around us, life always seems to be one move ahead. The path to a financially stable future may seem uncertain, but the best thing that you can do is assess your needs and lean into reliable sources of support. That being said, I hear how challenging this season might be, and I want you to know that I genuinely believe that better days are ahead. When the world feels unpredictable and instability shows up, remember this…

- You are worthy of peace – always. There is no shame in finding yourself in unpredictable circumstances. You are not to blame, and no fault can lie with you.
- You are more equipped for unpredictability than you think you are. As humans, we have a lifetime of experience navigating unaccounted-for eventualities. It is literally within our nature to evaluate what is going on around us and to adjust. Utilise your strengths and acknowledge the places where support may be helpful. Even when it feels like all hope of stability is gone, there is still a chance for things to be better than they are.
- Though unpredictability comes in all shapes and sizes, it is also a universal experience. You're never alone, and you don't have to manage this season on your own.

A Place of Refuge

(inspired by the prompt 'for a refugee')

When life tosses uncertainty up in the air, regardless of whether we are prepared for it, a safe refuge might feel a thousand miles away. Whether fleeing somewhere, someone, or something with little warning, nothing can prepare us for having to retreat out of fear or for lack of a place of safety – and nothing should have to. So many have been forced to seek refuge from circumstances they had no control over, with no choice but to imagine a place of safety from a dwelling of danger. If this uncertainty surrounds you now, I hope your need for refuge is met sooner than expected. While hope seems distant, it is not lost, and I hope you have the opportunity to seek it out and the courage to welcome it as it finds you.

For a moment, imagine a vision of refuge… what is it that you picture? Is the place you imagine somewhere known to you, or is it somewhere that exists only in your mind's eye? Does your place of refuge offer a sense of comfort, and can it promise a hope that upholds and sustains you? Refuge is intrinsic to us, so wherever your sanctuary may be, may its presence be a hope-filled promise to you – a mirage no more when you need its tangible comfort.

I know I can't know just how the search for refuge may have impacted you, but I know some of what it is like to seek refuge, even if my journey looked different from the way that yours does. Some people in my life feel like home; my place of refuge is found in those who surround me or who have left a piece of themselves with me. Their consistent, tangible presence is what brings me home from the darkest places my mind drifts to. May you, too, know an unfaltering refuge of having loved ones around you. I hope that wherever life finds you and however your story unfolds, you find safe refuge with all the certainty that you deserve.

A Revelation of Peace

(inspired by the prompt
'finding peace in the small things')

What does it mean to find peace? How do we recognise it and allow space for peace to exist? Is it possible to choose peace when overwhelm and anxiety appears to consume us? I imagine that I am asking many of the same questions that you are, so, honestly speaking, when it comes to finding peace, I'm still learning.

Peace appears to be one of those feelings that I yearn for, yet I wrestle with myself to experience it. There is sometimes an unspoken conflict in striving for peace. My longing for it robs me of the chance to feel it at all, something that I know I am not alone in feeling. In light of this, I'd encourage you to acknowledge and embrace peace in every moment where it finds you (even when the moment seems unworthy of note). I can appreciate that my words might seem vague here, so hear me out as in this letter I explore my own revelations about peace.

To find peace will mean something different to everyone. I think of peace as a state of inner calmness within the outer chaos and serenity found in the seemingly ordinary. To me, to find peace is to stumble across a rare opportunity to breathe, where it feels as though a breath should not be, but you have the capacity to take it anyway.

I guess when we find peace in the small things, we can also accept that peace doesn't just arrive at perfection. True peace doesn't come from everything falling into place or being just so. I imagine that peace is felt at its utmost depth when we need it most, and we need it most when things seem uncertain. When you make space for peace by seeing it every day in the small things, even at a time when it seems like it should be furthest from you, somehow, its magnitude is felt at a greater depth. Peace is a resting place that is not reliant on circumstance – ultimately because it becomes a daily choice rather than a constant benchmark to reach.

I know, and appreciate, that finding peace in the small things is easier said than done, but, just as I've known the wretched ache of anxiety and depression, I have also felt the safe arms of peace. To find peace is to choose to feel it. When the days of anguish tumble together, eventually there reaches a time where a subtle shift happens. Without even noticing it, you will find yourself in a calmer state. Having chosen to seek peace out, finding peace is then to acknowledge and embrace the simplicity of the everyday. In my experience, peace rests within us when we acknowledge what we can't control and instead focus on being – embracing the small things and perfectly timed peace. Peace has this ability to lace moments in all the necessary ways, seamlessly woven between our thoughts, feelings, and experiences.

I can't even begin to tell you how much I long for you to know that peace now. Though peace may seem a far-off truth from where you are at this moment, I'd love for you to take a minute to read these words that I have written. I hope that they bring a sense of comfort until peace is a choice that you feel ready to make and a feeling that you're ready to embrace.

Weary soul, between the lines, I hear your desire to find peace; the feelings of peace will fall upon you when you least expect them to. As it laces your heart and mind, I hope that it reveals itself to you in the small details of your comings and goings.

When all that surrounds you is moving ferociously, breathe a little deeper and remind yourself that even here it is possible to have peace rest within you. May it be evident in the storms that pass, the sun that shines, the sea that ripples, and in the dandelion clocks as their seeds whisp in the wind. I hope that peace is present with you in every season that you come through. Just as you can choose to see peace in the small things, joy too can be found – and hope is never far behind.

All I Know Now

(inspired by the prompt
'a letter to your past self about who you grow to be')

There are many things I wish I could share with my past self – hence this letter. It has been special to take a moment to share all I know now while thinking of Millie throughout the ages of becoming the woman she is today. Perhaps they'll mean something to you too.

To Millie at three,
your empathy will come into its own.
In time compassion will be your harnessed gift.

To Millie at five,
your innate desire for friendship is unique and special.
Love fiercely and unreservedly no matter the consequences.

To Millie at eight,
the same joy you see in others radiates through you.

To Millie at eleven,
dream 'impossible' dreams.
Create without striving for perfection.

To Millie at sixteen,
you'll trust yourself again.

To Millie at twenty,
though the path isn't linear,
wander until the way ahead appears clearer.

To Millie at twenty-four,
you're a work in progress.
but you're beginning to embrace who you are.

Chapter Five | The Power of Love
(Part I)

How Loved You Are

(inspired by the prompt 'how could someone love me?')

You ask, 'How could someone love me?'
My response is, 'How could someone not?'

Love, by definition, is a feeling of deep affection. Nowhere does love claim to be perfect, nor is it reserved for perfect people. We are all inevitably flawed. I don't believe there is a single being who cannot love or be loved. The truth is that I think we overcomplicate love. We try to second guess it, earn it, or deserve it but love just *is* – and that can be a beautiful thing.

You do not need to question whether you are loved. I write all these letters from a place of affection. As I write this now, I long for love to weave in amongst the lines. I hope that wherever this letter finds you, my love and care for you meet you where you are.

I may not know the full extent of your story, or even why you question *how* someone could love you, but I do know that you are worthy of feeling loved. I also know that no matter what has come before, or what lies ahead, you deserve to know love with certainty. Doubt has a way of robbing us of the assurance of the truth. This lack of assurance leaves us restless and trapped within the confines of what we can believe. Know that you are free to accept love in all its forms – rest in it and soak it up.

How widely, deeply, and profoundly loved you are.
That might feel like an odd thing to hear from a stranger,
but I know this love to be true.

The Face of Love

(inspired by the prompt
'love comes in many forms')

When I think of love, I see the faces of kind strangers, close friends, and my family. I simultaneously feel the weight – and the weightlessness – of what it is to fall deeply. I hear the sound of heartbreak and grief while also embracing resounding comfort and joy. I sense good intentions and the ever-changing motions of love in all its forms.

Love is within all of us; it is the beating heart of this life that we get to live. I find that love changes many things – trading loneliness for friendship, sorrow with joy, heartbreak with wholeness, and loss with life. Love threads itself between brokenness, creating beautiful things. In all forms, love can shift narratives and change the course of someone's life forever. We know love to be tangible, like in the touch of pinkie fingers or the spoken and unspoken exchanges with loved ones. I adore the way that our actions and reactions have the potential to be laced with love, even incidentally.

Embracing love completely, to some extent, is to also embrace the places where it feels difficult to love and be loved. In all its definitiveness, love is also reckless and uncertain. Somehow this is part of the great love stories that we come to tell. Love remains central to us, holding space for diversity and difference while celebrating what unifies and brings us together.

More than anything else, we are known for the way that we love. Fill your intentions with love; fill them up so that the face of love remains one that reflects something that has the potential to change the world for the better. Seek out the places where you can leave people better than you found them and strive to show yourself the same love that you exude. Open yourself up to receiving love and watch your world change for good.

The Significance of Friendship

(inspired by the prompt
'loving a friend')

We were designed to do life with one another. Being around other people can enrich our experiences of the day to day, in the highs, lows, and everything in between. Though friendships change and evolve, the power of friendship remains consistent, which is why it is something that I invest in. I could not be without some of the friendships I have formed throughout my life. It would be easy to use this space to attempt to eloquently speak of the love that I have for my friends onto the page, but they know who they are, and they know how much I love them, so instead, I want to use this space to talk about the significance of friendship.

Friendship is a relationship that is often overlooked and sometimes taken for granted. I firmly believe that friendship is just as meaningful as other relationships that we long for. I know that friendship is something that I value, and I am grateful to have known its tender touch in infinite ways throughout my life. From seasonal connections with individuals that I still hold dearly to timeless friendships that hold steadfast and true, I feel that I've been blessed with the gift of friendship immeasurably more than I could have imagined. Dear reader, my friend, my heartfelt wish is that you know the power of friendship – if not yet, then in days to come.

Friendship is a unique kind of love. When I think of some of my closest friends, I realise now that I see them more like family. We do life with our friends, taking them through the highs and lows of our existence. We encourage each other, celebrate each other's accomplishments as if they were our own, and take one another in. We do these things willingly, without obligation. In writing this, it has come to me: friendship, in essence, is a relationship that requires us to choose to love – a significant choice indeed.

When Connection Counts

(inspired by the prompt
'an interaction with someone that made you smile')

I love interacting with other people. Fleeting moments of interaction appear to conjure up a lightness in me, putting the pep in my step for the rest of my day. There is something humanely beautiful about connecting with one another that fulfils me. This prompt called for an interaction with someone that made me smile. While there are many that I could recall, one came strongly to the forefront of my mind – a moment that I hope will make you smile too…

10th October 2021
I went for a walk this morning. Sleep-filled eyes, beanie hat, and headphones – nothing special, right? A young child and their mum walked past me – she was skipping but that's beside the point although I appreciated her childlike zest. Having removed my headphones to greet them, I overheard 'Mummy, that lady looks really cool. I love her!'

To clarify, I've never been called 'cool' in my life! I don't know if she really thought I looked cool, but I was elated to say the least, though left pondering about her fondness for me. I couldn't quite believe that she thought that I was worthy of note. Then, it dawned on me. Even when I am bumbling along, finding my way and questioning my place, I can still be seen in a way that reflects strength, coolness (it would seem), and, above all – I am still worthy of love. If she could say it with such assurance, then surely, I can begin to believe it too.

To love is a powerful thing, but I wonder if we overthink it. She gave way for her love without a single ounce of reservation and without considering the impact it would leave. I have so much love and appreciation for that little girl, yet we may never truly know each other…

The Fullness of Love

(inspired by the prompts 'to someone who was betrayed' & 'to someone who betrayed in the past')

So many thoughts and feelings come to my mind when I begin to think about betrayal. From the cold harshness of the word itself to the memories of experiences where I could pinpoint that feeling, I find that nothing about betrayal is easy to articulate. Betrayal is complex, yet it is rarely spoken about. Loneliness can be stacked with shame – leaving the betrayed isolated when we need connection more than ever.

I hear that you've been hurt; I wish that I could have spared you from this. I know that I couldn't have, but I hope to provide some comforting words for navigating the betrayal that you've experienced. Wherever these words find you, know that you can find peace. May your heart heal, and may your soul be open to loving again.

Don't give up on love. Love will meet you where you are. It will surround you with a warmth that holds the broken pieces together and fuses them until the betrayal doesn't leave you feeling broken in the same way anymore. You are deserving of love, no matter how much the lies in your brain might choose to tell you otherwise. Love will find you, even here, in simple and beautiful ways.

Equally, don't give up on giving love. Loving isn't the reason that you were betrayed, though I appreciate that it would be easy to allow bitterness, fear, or the long-lasting aches of grief to keep you from loving again. It may not feel like the pain will ever leave, but it is possible to grow around it and move through such hurt when the time is right for you.

Let me reassure you that with time, you will find your sense of self again. You can choose to love once more, and you can choose to let it in. For those who have felt betrayed, be reminded that amongst your anger, resentment, and pain, there is space for grace.

However, this letter isn't only for the betrayed but also for those who know that they have betrayed others. This letter is not one of judgement. How could it be when I know that I, too, will have hurt people along the paths that I have travelled? Part of being human is that we are all inevitably flawed. Each one of us will have made mistakes that have negatively impacted those around us, whether intentional or otherwise.

Whatever transpired at the time of betrayal, I want you to know that I see you – worthy of the same love and grace as everyone else who has made mistakes in their relationships. It might not always feel like that is the case but, here and now, it is. Though an act of betrayal is challenging to unpack for all involved, I hope that amongst it all, your heart can return to a grounded place. Be humble, be kind, and, most of all, be as honest as possible. Remain empathic to those who have been impacted, for empathy appears to create a chain reaction of individuals who can hold space for one another. Grace can be healing in many ways, and wouldn't the world be a kinder place if we granted each other grace intentionally and without reservation in the same way that we love?

Forgiveness is just one characteristic of love, but I do believe that it is a central quality found in the fullness of love, not just forgiveness between people but also the forgiveness of oneself. Betrayal typically arises from places where love once was; if we know this to be true, then the same love can enable us to move forward. I hope that you will forgive yourself and make space for healing so that you might move forward and build relationships with others where love overrides all else. Along the way, I hope that you uncover peace at its greatest depth and that you experience love in all its fullness in the way that you deserve.

When We Come Together

(inspired by the prompt
'a love letter to family-like community')

There is something extraordinary about being part of a community. When we choose to surround ourselves with like-minded people who are with us and for us, a beautiful connection can form – one that I know to be lifesaving. Communities take those who might otherwise feel isolated and embrace them – a kindness that should never be underestimated – while being the perfect example of compassion. Such humanity is something I am thrilled to celebrate in this particular love letter. The words below are a celebration of such a community. They were first published as part of a personal essay to express my gratitude to the online chronic illness community. I believe that these words also belong here, as they express my love with raw, irreplicable clarity. If you are seeking out a family-like community, I hope it shows up with perfect timing. If you are someone who shares in the joy of being a part of a loving community, consider this letter both a thank you and a celebration of all that you are. I know the world would be a better place if we could all hold each other with such love.

Community means belonging.
It finds you as you are with no hidden agenda.
It seeks you in the shadows
*   and allows you to live boldly in the light.*

Community says, "I hear you, and I am with you".
It rallies: "You're not alone in this anymore.".
Community whispers: "Have courage! I see that this is hard.
Take one day at a time. I am here alongside you".

Community breathes gently:
"You are loved, valued, and accepted just as you are".

Chapter Six | To the One Who…

To The One Who Dreams of Somewhere New

(inspired by the prompt
'a letter to someone who dreams of somewhere new')

Life has a way of prompting us sometimes. Whether with subtle hints or a huge sign that cannot be denied, when the call for somewhere new falls upon us, it can be a daunting prospect (no matter how desired the change is). Occasionally, I'm grateful for life's nudge in a particular direction, such as when I took an extended break in London rather than just the intended day trip. I booked my hotels last minute (the morning that I caught the train), and it turned out to be just the place that I needed to be for some much-needed recuperation and Millie-time. The somewhere new in this instance was temporary, but the feeling of rest it gifted me was long-lasting.

At other times, life's prompts for somewhere new are a more nerve-wracking ordeal, particularly when it comes to making bolder decisions about our future. For me, the call to study in Liverpool was strong. It wouldn't have mattered what course I enrolled on or how things turned out, I knew I was being pulled in that direction for a reason. I am glad that I took the leap, even in the moments when it was hard to understand why I'd landed there.

I sense that you've dreamed of placing your feet upon new soil for a while now. In this prompt, I hear the yearning for somewhere new – an adventurous curiosity for a change in situation and surroundings. When you look up to the moonlit sky, the stars align and somewhere new is filled with peace and prosperity.

You can picture grounding yourself where your soul can rest; a place where the burden is light, and you can start afresh. Whether in your mind, on your doorstep, or around the world and back again, something new will take its place on your path when you are ready to embrace it. I hope you know that you have the strength to pursue the somewhere new in your heart.

I know the fear, and I appreciate the risks that come with trialling something new. Sometimes, I have been daring enough to leap (with a varied amount of success), but I, too, have retreated from my dreams at times. That is not to say that I am not proud of the occasions that I have strode out into the unknown, because I am, but I can acknowledge that there are opportunities that I have missed because the fear of failure drowned out all the positive potential and possibility.

Despite characteristically being risk averse, as I write this, I find that I only want to encourage you. I am frequently in awe of those who pursue their dreams, longings, and ambitions without hesitation – even without knowing the concrete details. There is something gallant about having the courage to see beyond what is known, and not just to step into it but to dream fervently and expectantly. A little nugget of wisdom for you – a piece of advice that I should refer to myself from time to time – is that I rarely regret the risks that I have taken when it has come to my dreams. Even when the stars have not aligned as I envisioned, I have gained from the places that I have been.

You might find that somewhere new falls in line with your vision; unless you try, you won't ever know what could have been. Just as this is true, I acknowledge that somewhere new may not work out for you the way you had hoped for, and that is okay too. It is perfectly alright to try things and make changes along the way. It is not a waste, and there should be no mention of inadequacy. I wish I had known this to be true much sooner than I did. I spent so much time avoiding risk, forever adamant that I would fall short, so I appreciate the bold mentality needed. However, know that there is always a way through and forward.

Newness requires the fiercest courage, but if life prompts you and you're able to take the opportunity, then why should you waste time worrying? Make wise decisions and informed choices, but don't allow doubt to rob you of the somewhere new that could offer you what you need.

To the One Who Is Feeling Lost

(inspired by the prompt 'feeling lost')

Sometimes I think we place too much pressure on ourselves to be in the 'right' place at the 'perfect' time. You might find yourself thinking about how a different decision would have taken you in the planned direction, or you might question the very place where you have ended up having reached your destination. However, perhaps you are not lost as such, maybe you are simply on a slight detour. At such a time, I would recommend that you toss out the old map (the sort that none of us knows how to read anyway) and get driving.

There is something about being lost that feels much better and brighter when we see it like a road trip! On a recent adventure with my pal Jess, we wound up on what would have appeared to be the wrong road. Grass grew along the middle, yet we were expecting to take a fairly main road from Devon to Cornwall. At a time when it would have been easy to panic, we turned the music up and followed the road until we had an inkling of where we were headed and ended up on a better road ahead than I had originally planned. Sure, there was a moment when we were concerned that we were about to spend nearly two hours on some remote tracks, but we had each other, and we knew that we would get to where we were destined to be.

I am a big advocate for altering perspective when you get a sense that things might not go your way. A change in viewpoint can help you realign to a place of security, despite the unknown, and enable you to trust in the process. I am someone who tries to be cautiously optimistic at every twist, turn, and setback (though I am the first to admit that I don't always succeed in having a positive outlook). Rest assured that we all get a little lost sometimes, but never so lost that we cannot find our way again or be found and pointed in the right direction. At the point where you are most lost, you are also at your closest to finding your way again (a truth I have learned to remind myself of often in my day-to-day life).

So, take in the glorious wake of day and watch it turn to dusk, and free yourself from the need to know exactly where you are going. Roll down those windows, smell the fresh dew drops, let the wind caress your face, and allow the weather to caress your skin (regardless of whether it is sun, rain, or snow)! Turn the music up a little louder, bosh out your favourite pair of sunglasses (we all have them, regardless of whether we look cool in them), and trust that the journey will take you exactly where you need to be. If, along the way, you want to pull over and change direction, that is okay! There is no correct way to arrive at your destination – so long as along the way you come to a place of peace at your journey's end.

To the One Who Seeks Rest

(inspired by the prompt 'exhaustion')

We were not designed to take in as much of the world at once as we appear to – fact. However, more so than ever, everything *around* us appears to demand our attention instantaneously and perfectly with little room for error. We live in a world where working tirelessly or having a gridlocked schedule is a norm and expectation – praised and admired with minimal consideration for the long-term impact. Exhaustion is becoming a universal feeling, so we each have something to learn from a conversation surrounding rest. I know this as someone who previously only felt worthy when teetering on the edge of burnout. If nobody has said this to you before, you do not have to prove your value through the act of doing.

Let me be the one to tell you that needing to rest is not a weakness because rest is a necessity – one that you are worthy of. Understand this – don't wait for a day to make itself available to you, but instead be intentional about making space for rest. Plan 'lazy days' and opportunities for recuperating your mind, body, and soul. Allow yourself the chance to rest in weightlessness and bask in the peace it affords you. You are enough as you are, and I hope that this encouragement will be a tangible reminder of this truth when exhaustion is upon you.

Finding Freedom from Addiction

(inspired by the prompt
'the struggle of addictive patterns')

In life, we battle addictions. The world in which we live is fuelled by the idea that we become addicted to what the world can offer us. From technology to gambling, battles with food, money, drink, or drugs, or an addiction to self-sabotage or bad relationships, there are a whole host of potential addictions that any one of us can face day to day. From the offset, I just want you to know that freedom from this addictive pattern is possible. Even if right now you don't know how you will ever reach the other side, hold on, for I believe you are never too far gone.

Addiction can feel like it is already one step ahead of you. It may leave you feeling hopeless and worthless yet completely bound into the cycle of wanting more. Addiction thrives on being all-consuming and may lie to you about what you are worth. I'm asking you to trust the process even when it feels like it is breaking you and lean into the love that surrounds you. When addiction tries to rob you of having a support system around you, remind yourself that you are worthy of love and worthy of recovery. When facing addiction, you do not shoulder the weight of it alone. There is support waiting for you with open arms, in the shape of friends, family, and communities, and there is no shame in asking for help.

You are not defined by the adversities that you have faced. They may be a part of you, and they may be a part of the story that you tell, but they are not all that people see in you. On those days when you doubt yourself, I want you to think about the people that you treasure in your life. Do you ever see others as less than because of their circumstances or experiences? You are not less than because of your addictive patterns. They are a part of you, and seem to rob the best parts of you, but you are still whole. Your lionhearted spirit is evident. It shows up in the quietest of whispers and the mightiest of roars – there is so much strength within you.

To the One Who Doesn't Feel Good Enough

(inspired by the prompt
'to the one who doesn't feel good enough')

Dear reader, I hear the pain in your voice, perhaps because I know the voice of self-doubt well. That being said, it turns out that our brains aren't always to be trusted when it comes to the truth about ourselves, so let me tell you the truth today. You needn't even be *good* enough, for *you* alone are enough. Just as you are, imperfections and all, *you are enough*.

Perhaps no one has ever said that to you before. It is a privilege to be the one to tell you now. Nothing that you do or say could make you more or less worthy. No matter what has gone before or what there is to come, you are free to welcome in the self-acceptance, respect, and love that tells you every day that you, yes *you,* are enough.

One day, you will feel good enough.
It might not be today.
It may not be tomorrow,
but one day you will feel you are enough - just as you are.

You won't vie for the love and approval of others.
You won't wonder if you could have been more
or should have been less.
You won't wonder if life would have looked a little different,
and you won't regret what was.

You will flourish,
free from the weight of inadequacy.
For, one day, you will know that you are enough.

To the One Learning to Love Their Body

(inspired by the prompts
'making peace with the way that I look' and
'a letter on how to be confident in my own skin')

Life is too short not to make peace with the way that you look – fact – but I am aware that simply stating that won't change years of societal pressures on the value of appearance. Learning to love your body is one heck of a journey, one that most of us embark upon over a lifetime. I, too, am learning to love my body and find confidence in it through its ever-changing state. Body confidence certainly isn't a destination, but it is a mindset that we can put into practice as and when we need it, and it is a conversation that we can have that reduces the isolation felt when we run into a lack of peace about the way that we look.

So much of what I have learned about loving my body has come from those around me. Whether inspired by strangers on the internet or absorbing the kindness expressed to me throughout life's highs and lows, the wisdom I have accumulated concerning body image is far broader than I had ever considered. Words of wisdom have cropped up from all over the place, whenever and wherever they found me – some of which I thought I would share with you...

1. *'Smile in the mirror when you catch yourself looking.'* This simple action has made such a difference to me. Scientifically, smiling is known to reduce stress due to the signal sent to our brains. In a crisis of confidence, this tiny pearl of wisdom has brought me joy even through tears in a state of paralysis about what to wear or what I look like.
2. *'What is perfect?'* This phrase was often said to me by a counsellor I was privileged to work with. She reminded me, without even realising, that I had the opportunity to make peace with myself over my body by rejecting unattainable 'perfection'.

3. *'You are more than the body that houses you.'* While I am learning that there is so much to appreciate about my body, I have always known that I couldn't rely on my changing appearance or unreliable brain to find a sense of worth in the way that I look. This meant having to uncover an unshakeable confidence that remained constant no matter how my physique, style, or ability to function changed. My kindness, gentle nature, and empathy cannot be reflected in a mirror, but they are essential parts of who I am.
4. *'Pretty and mess are not mutually exclusive.'* A comment that has become a foundation by which I have built some semblance of self-worth! I found a quiet liberation in the knowledge that I didn't have to look like I had it all together to be loved as I was – that I could embrace every inch of who I am and still believe myself to be beautiful. While there are times when it feels like my body is failing me or is not up to the standards of the world, I can still find beauty in the way I look and in who I am.
5. *'It is not shameful to not appear beautiful.'* The peace these words have afforded me, to acknowledge that my 'lack of beauty' felt shameful, has been a game changer for my perspective on body image. We came into this world without a warped view of the space we could take up in this world. Why can't we embrace that same freedom now? When we free ourselves from the lies that we have allowed ourselves to believe, it is amazing what can happen!

Beloved reader, there are far more interesting things about you than the way you look, but in case you need that reminder today, I love how much beauty there is in the full essence of who you are. Take the time to appreciate the nuance in your uniqueness – love it and the soul that gives it life, and you'll uncover the confidence that has been within you all along. We are on this journey of self-acceptance together. One day, we will see the same beauty in ourselves that we admire in others.

To the One Who Is Healing

(inspired by the prompt,
'how do I live after existing in survival?')

When I received this prompt, I couldn't help but be in awe of your boldness because, in my experience, the struggle with a journey of healing is one that we don't often share with others. I find that we tend to share only the 'before and after' snapshots, or a highlight reel, of what was experienced – forcing us into the belief that it is not possible to heal, survive, and live simultaneously at a given time. Healing can often feel messy, and it isn't as straightforward as we make it sound on reflection. In recognition of that, I just wanted to reach out and personally thank you for your vulnerability. I imagine that there will be others who identify with the idea of existing in survival during a time of healing (me included). Because of you and your courageous effort to speak out, they will feel less isolated.

As I came to write this letter, I found myself questioning what it means to survive and to live. I hope that sharing this exploration of healing will encourage you to be curious about life in a different way. I hear the pull of asking what it means to live – but please, hear me out.

To heal can be defined as a process by which something broken is made good, so, what if surviving and healing were evidence of living? Healing can begin now that you take your next breath… in… and out… do you see? You're living, breathing, surviving, and healing – all in one moment, as simple as breathing.

I appreciate that patience is needed for the art of healing and the science of restoration. In this season of waiting, know that you are no more or less worthy than the breath you took before, just in a different place than you will be with your next exhale. Healing doesn't have to be this big miracle moment; healing is just as present in the stillness and the murmur of the belief that better days are coming – while you are free to make peace with where you are now.

Boundless Truths for a Housebound Day

(inspired by the prompt
'a letter to someone who is housebound')

Dear reader, I know there is no way for me to know exactly where life finds you right now. Though I long for the world to open itself up to you, I sense the unsaid struggle in finding yourself housebound. Know that every piece of me longs to extend a gentle touch of friendship in your direction. For every moment of lightness that is kept out by the walls that surround you, may the subtle light from small joys brighten the space around and within you.

Whether the days are solitary, or they fall one after the other, my heartfelt hope is that you can find some comfort in this letter that I write to you. If your mind deceives you or the day-to-day moments feel like they are too much to bear, here are ten boundless truths for those housebound days; may they glow the lightness of what is true into those darkened spaces.

1. Though your struggles aren't always seen and the things you endure aren't always known, I see you and I love you. I see the beautiful essence of who you are.
2. You are free to take up space as you are. Though the world may struggle to make that evident, this fact does not change. I hope that compassion is something that resoundingly brightens your days; you are worthy of everything good.
3. Your best is always good enough. If anything, or anybody, ever tries to tell you differently, prompt yourself with the truth that just existing is a momentous miracle.
4. Your worth is not changeable, neither is the love felt for you.
5. The balance of hope and acceptance can be hard to find. It is okay if there are times when this balance feels just out of reach; I am hopeful that unexplainable peace will find its way to you on the days that the balance threatens to unsteady. You do not have to manage your circumstances

perfectly, just with as much self-compassion as you can muster up, and your whole fusion of feelings is welcome here.
6. It is okay to grieve for the way you thought things should have or would have been. You do not have to sugar-coat painful experiences with silver linings. Your feelings (including anger or grief) are welcome to come to the forefront. I wish I could protect you from the pain you might be feeling. Just know that in these moments, my arms are open wide to you, and my heart is with you through every peak and valley.
7. You have never been nor could ever be a burden. When the weight you carry is too much to shoulder alone, lean into the support that is given to you. What you are facing may feel burdensome, but *you* are not a burden.
8. You need not be ashamed. While your feelings of fear, anguish, doubt, or frustration are valid, shame has no place in the situations that surround you. Grant yourself the grace that you would so freely give to someone else in your position.
9. Make space for joy – the kind of gladness not based on circumstance. It is the joy found in the smaller details that will see you through this challenging season. You will learn to tune in to the joyfulness that surrounds you in astonishing ways you are yet to foresee.
10. Remain present while feeling free to escape the confines of the walls around you with pure escapism. If the thought of tomorrow feels like it is too much to imagine, ground yourself in whatever brings you comfort: a favourite song, a seaside shell, a cosy blanket, or the way the sunlight dances around a room. Beloved stranger, you're not alone, even when the loneliness aches more than you knew was possible. As quickly as overwhelm came, it can go, and I hope that the light pours into places that seem too overshadowed by the darkness.

To the One Who Is Grieving

(inspired by the prompt
'grief')

The experience and impact of grief are far broader than we might imagine at first. Sadly, grief is the cost of living and loving – a tough price to pay – but I have come to consider that choosing to live and love is something I can never regret (even when this is painful).

Numerous circumstances may leave us grieving; unfortunately, there is no rule book for finding our way through a season like this. However, I do believe at times like these, there is value in knowing that while our grief is valid, we can trust and believe that we're not alone…

To the one grieving for a loved one, I want you to know that each seemingly conflicting feeling of grief is welcome here. Ride the good days and bad days with their waves of whatever comes and know that the weight of this loss is not just yours to bare. Whether it has been weeks or years, your grief has a safe, soft place to land. The love you shared with the one you lost will remain etched in your mind and on your heart forever.

To the one grieving in anticipation of loss, how I wish I could spare you this heart-breaking pain. My friend, precious one, when the grief feels intimidating or too much to even fathom, remain present where you can and lean into cherishing life as it happens.

To the one grieving security, you don't have to face this season alone. Uncertainty may rob you of peace of mind, but it needn't to when you have the right people around you.

To the one grieving amid illness or for plans that you'd made, remember that you have not missed out on what was meant for you. Though this season is looking different from how you'd once imagined it and the road ahead couldn't be further from what you'd planned it to be, each day can still be filled with a lightness destined for you.

To the one grieving for a life you once knew and to the one grieving a life you've never known, while the unexpectedness of the day's comings and goings are unsettling to you right now, I hope that you find a rhythm that is steady and secure. There is untapped potential in what today has to offer you; may its subtlety be a relief to your body and soul.

To the one grieving a broken relationship, though grieving for something or someone, we can be left grieving in other parts of our lives too. You may grieve for who you were before, the plans that were, or the life you hoped to build. I hope that you find the strength to claim what is yours and rebuild from the ground up in beautiful, unimaginable ways.

To the one grieving for dreams that once felt within reach, I foresee new dreams breathed in you. Whether they echo imaginings from childhood fantasies or come about with little reason, there are infinite dreams to dance amongst, and you deserve your place within them.

To the one grieving without knowing just what you are grieving for, your experience of this tumultuous feeling is just as valid. It is possible to experience both grief and peace if you'd allow restlessness to be expressed. If or when it begins to make sense, may you be surrounded by those who can enable you to find your way back to a place of sanctuary.

To the one grieving in this season, you do not face this grief alone. While the loneliness aches and overwhelm washes over you, please know that I am here. May there be comfort in knowing you're surrounded by my thoughts and my love – they are never far away.

We're in this together –
we'll hold space for each other
and find a way through no matter what tomorrow brings.

To the One Who Is Embracing Change

(inspired by the prompt
'to the one who is embracing change')

How wonderful to hear that you are embracing change in this season and that you are opening yourself up to the possibility of exciting things before you! When we are not in control, change can feel a little threatening, but when we are craving change and are free to embrace it, I find that there is liberation in the prospect. Perhaps the anticipated changes are big and evident, but perhaps they are smaller – both are equally as filled with potential.

Often when we seek out change, we have a vision of where we would like to wind up, but it is important to allow the space for a plan to fall into place as opposed to having a set blueprint for the pathway forwards. Everything we do comes with an element of surprise, but without taking a leap into the unknown, you could rob yourself of the opportunity to land somewhere special.

Perhaps your desire for change could come about in ways you were yet to imagine. There is something within you that believes that things can be different – far from the predictable life you are living. Embracing change requires bravery; this same courageousness will carry you through any adversities you face. Embracing change, to some extent, is about embracing the uncertainty of a changing season. From my dabbles in the game of change, what I can say is that I have learned so much from experiencing the unexpected. You realise that it is possible to find goodness in your circumstances and embrace change in a whole new way...

When I look up and notice the colours of the leaves, I observe the way the colours change. Instead of growing and falling straight from the trees, the leaves embrace seasonal changes. They take the opportunity to turn slowly from green to orange to russet red before they land upon the ground, and you, too, will be all the richer for embracing a *season* of change.

Chapter Seven | Music for the Soul

Music for the Soul

(inspired by the prompt 'Music')

So many things spring to mind with the prompt of 'music'. Having studied music at university, my mind is filled with memories of lectures on The Beatles and attempts at songwriting online. However, there is something far more intimate about the kind of music that I truly love, the kind of music that has fed my soul since I was a young girl singing along to cassettes in the backseats of my parents' respective cars. By definition, music is the production of 'form, harmony, and expression of emotion' (Concise Oxford Dictionary, 2021). This definition broadens the horizon for us when we are prompted by the word 'music' itself.

Music can be found all around us, which reminds me instantly of nature. The music of my soul is unearthed in birdsong, heard in waves disturbing pebbly beaches and the crunch of leaves beneath my feet in autumn. There's warmth in the crackling of fire and expressiveness in claps of thunder as it rains. Nature has a restorative quality in the melodies it breathes out, something poignant – indescribable in many ways. Just as this is true, I get a sense of drive and rhythm from life's daily soundtrack. An enjoyment of music can be found in the chatter in coffee shops, the whistling window cleaner, and the pitter-patter of feet across the playground at lunchtime. It's found in gentle sneezes or the use of sign language and agreeing sounds between strangers. The music of my soul is the accumulation of simple sounds and silence – the purest form of music that goes unnoticed, but we would be lost without it.

Music making is an innate part of human nature and free-flowing art at its best – a beautiful thing when you think about it. How wonderful to play a tiny part in the world's largest orchestra. I hope that you, too, make music in creative ways and find your place in it all.

You've Got Rhythm

(inspired by the prompt
'dancing to the beat of your own drum')

Having watched *Strictly Come Dancing* religiously since some of the earliest seasons, I was thrilled to find children's ballroom and Latin classes in a local church hall when I was nine. From then on, I regularly attended dance classes in one form or another up until I was nineteen. I loved the way that dance made me feel, and my love for it only grew.

Led by my passion for dance, I decided that I wanted to pursue a dance course at university. I spent the months between accepting the unconditional offer post-interview and freshers' week dreaming of the experience – completely bewildered, admittedly, that I had even been accepted onto the course. I think I was most excited about having the chance to grow into the confident unapologetic dancer I had always dreamed of being. I'm not ashamed to say that this didn't quite work out as I had planned…

Classes began and I was immediately taken aback by how quickly I doubted myself. Don't get me wrong, I'd had feelings like that before but never as strongly. As I danced through the initial classes, I found myself doing a double take at the girl looking back at me in the mirror. I wasn't surprised by the flaws in my dancing, but I was staggered at how quickly I fixated on them rather than the feeling of being on the dance floor.

To me, the mirror reflected a lack of strength in my body, weakness in my technique, and a fading passion for something that had given me so much joy. Despite a compelling love for dance and a genuine drive to succeed, I couldn't see past my shortcomings, leaving me in a bit of a quandary about how I would move forward.

That same evening, alone, I found my way back to the dance studio. Though ashamed of my faltering confidence, I wanted to puzzle things out.

Head hung low, eyes firmly fixed on the ground, I removed my shoes, pulled the blinds down to cover the mirrors, and made my way across the studio. 'Thursday' by Jess Glynne had recently been released and had quickly become my anthem of the season, so I plugged in the aux and turned the volume up.

As I trusted the movements, my heart opened, and I danced without a single ounce of reservation. At that moment, I made the difficult decision that I was going to move away from following dance as a profession. After all, dance was a sacred place where I could truly be myself, and somehow the mirrors in front of me robbed me of that experience. I had a feeling that I had made the right decision, despite the heartbreak it was causing me, but I also vowed to continue dancing fervently and passionately.

I have found that I most enjoy dancing when I can take to the floor alone – dancing to the music but ultimately dancing with movements that are completely my own so that I am free to embrace my unique sense of rhythm and style. Dance will always be a central part of who I am. I even relish the joy of the occasional dance class from time to time. At least when I return to the dance floor now, I have the strength to remember that the way that dance moves me is far more important than what those around me think of me or the flaws that one could point out in a studio mirror.

While I can't change some of the decisions I made based on the lies I had told myself about not looking good enough, or not feeling okay to dance freely, I move forward by making choices rooted in truth (and in doing so, I can share these words of wisdom with you too). I have come to believe that dancing to the beat of our own drum is a choice that we get to make and that this concept isn't just limited to the dance floor. You are welcome to lay down the limitations that you place on yourself, and you are free to embrace the rhythm within you. These days, I tell myself, 'Dance now, think later – or better still, don't think about it at all!'

What Baking Can Do

(inspired by the prompt 'waitress themed')

In October 2019, I had the joy of watching *'Waitress'* (starring Lucie Jones, David Hunter, and Joe Sugg). The music, written by Sara Bareilles, sensationally holds the story together. From start to finish, Emma and I were in tears as we watched Jenna's story unfold – the joy of baking proving to be a turning point for the character. Baking is Jenna's way out of an abusive relationship as a pie-making contest changes the course of her life, alongside the kindness of others. Though a fictional story, it is amazing what baking can do.

Baking creates a remarkable buzz. Internationally, we all have our traditions surrounding the baking that we do. In the UK specifically, baking is often in the media (across magazines, cookbooks, and the TV). *The Great British Bake Off* marks the beginning of autumn by bringing the nation together to witness some of the best amateur bakers that we have to offer. From the comfort of our sofas, we turn into bread experts as we watch Paul shove his thumb into underproved loaves. While the show brings many of us light and laughter, shows like these also bring the real-life impact of baking to the forefront. Whether it provides the bakers with a sense of achievement, escapism, or a creative outlet, the art of baking is special.

Thinking about baking floods my senses entirely. My mind is filled with the numerous kitchens I have baked in, those I have baked with, and those I have baked for. I live for the nostalgia of using ancient glass bowls and electric hand whisks. I most enjoyed baking with my cousin Sarah using traditional family recipes (mainly because we loved listening to accolades of 'that's just how mum would make it'). Sarah bakes with a perfect balance of precision and instinctiveness. Shortbread was our speciality, using our gran's delicious family recipe. I thought I would share the joy of this with you.

The MacPherson Scottish Shortbread Recipe

<u>Ingredients</u>

- 8 oz salted butter (room temperature)
- 4 oz caster sugar (a little extra to dust)
- 8 oz plain flour
- 4 oz cornflower

<u>Special Equipment</u>

- Swiss roll tin

<u>Method</u>

1. Preheat the oven (160 °C conventional oven / 140 °C fan oven).
2. Cream the butter and sugar together until fully mixed.
3. Combine the plain flour and cornflower in a separate bowl and add to the creamed mix two ounces at a time. The final mixture should resemble breadcrumbs.
4. Gather the mix together into a dough.
5. Grease your Swiss roll tin and dust the tin with flour.
6. Press the dough down into the tin. Flatten and smooth the dough out into the four corners of the tin.
7. Using a fork, gently create a regular arrangement of holes in the dough.
8. Bake in the oven for thirty minutes.
9. Sprinkle a little excess sugar and, using your fork, remake the holes before baking for a final five minutes.
10. Cut the shortbread into biscuits while still hot and leave in the tin until cool.
11. Enjoy!

While baking within the family is a cherished memory for me, baking allowed me to form relationships with others, some of whom I never met. Whether bringing baked goods to a gathering with friends or baking for strangers, I found that baking brought me closer to the people around me.

In my third year of university, I lived in a studio apartment. Given that Liverpool was placed in a tier three lockdown as I arrived, there weren't many ways to get to know the people in the neighbouring flats. That being said, I enjoyed leaving boxes of baked goods on the neighbours' doorsteps during this season, and before long, they were leaving little cakes and even loaves of bread at my door too. The small interaction of sharing baked goods between us felt special, and it connected us in ways I hadn't appreciated that I needed. Many of those I lived amongst that year I never saw the faces of, but we left handwritten notes scoring the bakes out of ten, and there was something so beautiful about how baking brought us together. I even had the opportunity to try some quite incredible traditional fortune cookies!

In this same season, my friend, Sophie, brought me some banana bread. We all remember the infamous lockdown banana cakes! We'd only ever met via Zoom call, but her kindness in reaching out gifted me a friendship that lifted me in this season. She was incredibly complimentary of my caramel shortbread, bringing out the best in me by building my confidence and showcasing just how baking could bring me closer to people.

When I think about what baking has done for me, I just want to encourage everybody to find what joy they can get from it. Whether it's an opportunity like Jenna, a cosy autumnal watch like *The Bake Off*, or family nostalgia and connection, there is so much that a little mix of ingredients can offer us. With a little sugar, butter, and flour, it's amazing what baking can do.

The Sound of Laughter

(inspired by the prompt 'laughing')

Laughter is one of my favourite sounds. I love the infectiousness of it and the way that each giggle, snort, chuckle, chortle, and guffaw is unique yet builds this beautiful choir and cacophony of sound. I laugh easily and once I have the giggles; I can't stop. My friends will vouch for the fact that I spent plenty of time working out how best to cover a laugh during lectures on Zoom (laughing behind a mug of tea became my preferred method).

For a little while, I would get a bittersweet feeling when I laughed – like I was somehow undeserving of feeling *so* much joy that it could burst out of me. The bittersweetness would come from wanting to catch the laughter with both hands, though I still felt unworthy of the joy that laughter brought me. I often worried that it was disingenuous to be struggling and then be joking around too. It wasn't until recently that I realised I am not alone in these types of feelings. Some people, for example, find this kind of pain in laughing after they lose someone close to them or in a season of depression. I remember this bittersweet feeling being one of the hardest things I have ever experienced, for what is laughter without the joy that comes with it?

I hope the resounding sound of laughter fills your soul. I hope that your eyes glisten with an indescribable energy and that you become so caught up in it that everything else fades away. On the bad days, I hope that the lightness of laughing reaches into the darkness and provides a warming glow through your mind and your body. I hope that there are days when you laugh without reservation – a big belly laugh that rolls around you and fulfils you.

Make space for the light,
and the darkness will loosen its grip.
You are worthy of joy even when you don't believe yourself to be.

Whispered Words Of Wisdom

(inspired by the lyrics from The Beatles' 'Let It Be')

Heavily influenced by my dad's music taste, The Beatles are a band that I have been familiar with since I was young. As a kid, I can't say that I was always thrilled with endless car journeys filled with their music, but I was intrigued, and I enjoyed our not-so-perfect harmony renditions of their songs. My dad seemed to be at his happiest when he was watching his children appreciating and celebrating the music that he loved. Over time, I grew to love their music – 'Paperback Writer' being a favourite song of mine. We found so much joy in belting Beatles hits at the top of our lungs, even when we didn't understand the weight behind their lyrics or the complexities of the music that we had the privilege of listening to.

That being said, my favourite thing about The Beatles isn't necessarily their music, although I have now come to appreciate how special it is. *My favourite thing about The Beatles is seeing the way that other people love them, their music, and the stories associated with them.* A wander around Liverpool's city centre, The Beatles Story exhibition, or the Abbey Road Studios will tell you all you need to know about the legacy they left.

When I spoke to my dad about The Beatles, he said, 'Saying that you *like* The Beatles is a bit like saying that you *like* your children. With The Beatles, it is love – a deep, unconditional love.' I'll admit that it surprised me a little to hear him speak so poetically about the way that The Beatles had moved him, which in turn moved me. He went on to say, 'The Beatles are a more familiar and integral part of my life than any material thing, yet they can surprise and delight me with each new listen. They weave themselves into the lives of my children, just as they wove themselves into mine; their words belong to all of us.

The Beatles are completely accessible, yet their appeal defies all rational explanations. They went on to define a generation and are as relevant and influential today as they were sixty years ago.'

This prompt called for a letter inspired by the song 'Let It Be'. This song, too, is a favourite Beatles' song of mine. The memorable refrains come to mind first and then the depth of the rest of the song floods into being. Writing this letter inspired me to give 'Let It Be' a more intentional listen. It is safe to say that I wasn't disappointed.

Music can be interpreted in so many ways. Being a musician myself, I could talk for hours about the technicalities of this song; however, it seems more important to talk about the emotional impact. 'Let It Be' has comforted individuals for generations with its thoughtful lyrics and simple melody. 'Let It Be' feels like it was written by a kind heart – it is like a warming mug of tea after a morning in the snow. There is something maternal and gentle in its spirit that makes time stand still for just a moment. Ultimately, 'Let It Be' is a tale of finding light in the darkness; it could almost be a call to action to lay down our burdens. The writer of this Beatles classic reflects on his personal experiences. Paul McCartney evaluates the role of perspective at a time when his troubles mounted up, again meeting the listener where they are with empathy and compassion, reassuring the listener that they, too, can put their troubles aside.

Isn't it beautiful that some music appears to make an impact that is wider than notes over the stereo? Consider allowing the music around you to comfort and console you. You might not find yourself reaching for The Beatles in your hour of need, but through their music, it is possible to see the impact that music can have on individuals and communities. It is a gift!

'And when the broken-hearted people,
living in the world agree,
there will be an answer,
let it be'

(The Beatles, 1970)

Millie's Playlist

(inspired by the prompt 'your ten favourite songs'*)*

Anyone who knows me personally will know that I am an avid music lover. My music playlists are eclectic: everything from McFly and TV show soundtracks to Motown and nostalgic tunes from the 2000s! As I write this letter, I find myself wondering what kind of music you like and dislike. I wonder if your showerhead receives the same sell-out arena concert each morning that mine does.

When I started having difficulties with my mental health, music took on a renewed role in my life. I began to love the way that music made me feel, embracing the way it moved people in different ways yet united us in indescribable ways. I loved how it helped me find myself and sit with my feelings while also taking me away to somewhere new. I hope that music provides as much of an escape for you as it does for me. Turn it up loud and let it flow through you. Let it change the atmosphere around you, allow it to remind you of moments in time that have come before, and let it build your sense of anticipation for what is to come. Music can transport you to some place new, or it can meet you exactly where you are. Let it move you, ground you, and capture you. Listen to it alone, in a crowded and busy room, or get out to a local gig and fall in love with independent music makers. It doesn't matter how, when, why, or what – just embrace music in new ways, and you may just find it has an unexpectedly profound impact on you and your life.

My ten favourite songs could easily change from day to day. My favourite music depends on the season I'm in at the time and what is most moving me to engage with or escape from my feelings. Here, I have tried to pick ten songs that have remained firm favourites for me throughout my life and that have moved me in different ways. I probably could have written an entire book on my favourite songs alone!

I love that someone has asked me to do this. Maybe you might find space to write out your top ten favourite songs for me to check out! However, for now, I leave you with this…

1. 'Dancing Queen' (Abba)

2. 'On My Way' (Phil Collins)

3. 'Fighting For Me' (Piano Version) (Riley Clemmons)

4. 'Landslide' (Fleetwood Mac)

5. 'Freedom! '90' (George Michael)

6. 'You Can Call Me Al' (Paul Simon)

7. 'Fearless' (Taylor's Version) (Taylor Swift)

8. 'Somewhere Only We Know' (Keane)

9. 'This Year's Love' (David Gray)

10. 'I'm A Believer' (Smash Mouth)

Chapter Eight | Open When….

Open When Your Heart Feels Heavy

(inspired by the prompt 'open when your heart feels heavy')

Hey, you, I hear that the heaviness of it all appears to be resting on your shoulders and weighing on your heart right now. An unexplainable sadness burdens you and seeps its way into each part of your body. You exhale, hoping the weight will ease but instead, the ache deepens. It's okay to sit with these feelings for a while – after all, you're not alone now. I'm here.

Our hearts hold many things; they hold the love we feel, the joy we share, the grief we experience, and the life within us. Each beat is another lived moment and yet another thing for our hearts to carry. Our hearts take on a lot, and before we know it, we are left overwhelmed by the weight of it all. It can feel like a rock sitting on your chest, unmoveable and unbreakable.

Sometimes I lie on my bed, looking out of the skylight at the stars, the feeling drained from my body. The next morning, I stand at the bay window and say, 'Today, we try again. One second, one minute, one moment at a time.' Life isn't always as simple as waking up and feeling better than the day before, I know, but what I'm trying to say is that each day is a new opportunity for hope to find a way through the heaviness.

Dear reader, with a little time, the weight will begin to lift; it will not weigh this heavy on your heart forever. A friend of mine says to me often, 'This too shall pass' – they have it tattooed on their arm. I love that it doesn't shy away from the fact that life can be difficult. We can feel like we are dealing with one thing after another. However, much like the trials you've already come through and the challenges you *will* overcome, this feeling of heaviness, too, will pass. Maybe not today or tomorrow, but it *will* pass. A heart can never be too burdened by life that it cannot hold space for love, a truth I am believing for you every step of today.

Open When the Seasons Change

(inspired by the prompt
'open when the seasons change')

A cold whisper echoes in the first light of the day. There is an icy crunch beneath nature's feet, and the shifting sunlight glows warmth to thaw the bitter chill. Robins peck at the damp soil as the ice melts, before retreating to the safety of the treetops, a cosy nest awaiting them.

I find myself wondering what the winter season brings for you. Winter can be a challenging season, even at the best of times when the Christmas excitement comes and goes. When the short days fly past and longer nights linger, it might feel difficult to see the light through the darkness. I find joy in the coloured fairy lights and cosy spaces and hold out for the spring days to follow. While you wait for the seasons to change, I hope you find a safe nest to rest in.

Dark clouds turn to white, grey skies turn to blue, and green creeps onto the scene once again. Flowers are in bloom and begin to open. Swallows and swifts appear in their thousands, returning home in anticipation of warmer weather. April showers create puddles for jumping in, and the May bank holiday opens us up to the possibility of spring's arrival.

The least predictable of the seasons – spring. In each season there are moments of beauty to be found, and the same can be true of the seasons in your life. Hope casts out fear of uncertainty and sees you celebrating in the wake of possibility and unpredictability. Spring reminds me that there is more than what we can see. It's a season of growth, even if it is slow and steady.

Holidays and staycations. Summer fruit in season – sweet, juicy, and homegrown. Some days, the sun radiates the joy of the season. At times, the humid thunderstorms arrive, and we hide inside peering behind the blinds as drops of rain trickle down the window. As Brits, we tend to spend months longing for summer. Then it arrives and we crave a cosy night by the fire!

Summer feels like the season where we see the least amount of change, but everything does appear to get a little brighter. The greens are more vibrant, the blues deeper than before, and we find ourselves amongst the thick of it all in the best ways. Some might feel the pressure of the perfect summer body or Instagram feed, but ultimately, when the summer season enters, it serenades us with life as we love it. We experience days that are familiar yet brand new.

Crisp leaves litter the forest floors and autumn fires warm the cooling wind. The beaches are emptier but not empty – filled with locals rather than those on holiday. Wavemakers, den builders, dreamers, and chance takers revel in the changing season. Auburn colours and softer tones come through, the low sun casting a sun-kissed glow on whatever it touches.

Autumn speaks to me, surrounding me with a love for the outdoors. We get excited over coffee; although I don't quite understand the hype of a spiced pumpkin latte. Change might be expected, but that doesn't always make it easy. Some dread the darker mornings and early evening nightfall. It is okay to find the changing season challenging. I hope that you find sparks of something autumnal to brighten up the spaces that feel lightless.

Winter, spring, summer, and fall – an array of colours and changing sensations. Abandoned soils flourish and adventure awaits those who are brave enough to embrace the change.

The earth provides this perfect reminder that seasons change. There can be moments when the seasons bring grief and loss or pain and heartache. Just as this is true, the seasons can also bring expectancy and fulfilment, joy, and hope like never before.

Open When You Cannot Sleep

(inspired by the prompt
'open when you cannot sleep'*)*

We've all experienced those moments of counting how many hours of sleep we'd get if we fell asleep right away and that sinking feeling when we realise it isn't as many as we'd have liked it to have been. I imagine if you've turned to this letter then you are looking for something different from the tried-and-tested sleep remedies. I like the smell of lavender as much as the next person, but sometimes it just doesn't seem to be all that effective. So, I thought I would write you a note of cosy comforts to keep you company in your sleepless time of need.

Whatever is keeping you up, I hope that this letter permits you to have the most restful night available to you. A restful night might not feel as beneficial as a sleep-filled one, but you'd be treating yourself with kindness to take the opportunity to truly rest whenever possible.

Though the dark hours of the night can feel lonely, it is not just you in this space. Beneath the moon and the stars, there are others of us feeling as you do. I find it reassuring to know that the loneliest needs can sometimes be met just by knowing that we are never truly alone. When the 3 a.m. anxiety sets in and you find yourself watching the clock, breathe deeply and remind yourself that you are seen, even in the dimmest of lights – remember that things may look brighter in the morning. You are allowed to find a place of rest without knowing all the answers; you do not have to shoulder the weight of tomorrow before it has arrived. In this moment, let go of achieving the 'perfect' night's sleep. You will get as much sleep as you get, and somehow, I know that you will make it through the next day with everything that you need. Provisions will be made, and grace will pave the way.

Open When The Sun Is Rising

(inspired by the prompt,
'write a letter when the sun is rising')

I catch the pink hues glowing through the cracks on either side of the blinds. I sit watching from the foot of my bed waiting in anticipation for the light to change. Ludovico Einaudi plays through the speaker, the sound of the birds outside chiming in from time to time. The melodies lead and the harmonies follow closely behind before becoming intertwined in perfect unison. The shower calls but I want to savour the weightlessness of it all for a little while longer.

After a short while, I get up from my bed and shuffle to the window. My sleep-filled eyes blink blearily, trying to bring the world into focus. I pull open the blinds a little further, inhaling one long deep breath. The darkened spaces are illuminated by the kiss of the golden beams, stretching into places I cannot reach. My mind feels clearer, though I can't explain why.

Watching on, I breathe slow but heavy breaths as the colours change and there is nothing but blue skies to be seen. After a short while, I turn away from the window to see the room bathed in sunlight.

Today, I find myself wondering if you've been dreaming of or dreading the arrival of a new day. I suppose at times it is possible to experience these feelings simultaneously. Whatever has been and whatever is to come, I hope that with the next sunrise you breathe a little deeper and feel the weightlessness with me – even if it is just for a moment.

I hope you soak up the feeling of the light changing – pink to orange and orange to the bluest skies. A fresh cup of coffee awaits you, and there is a blank canvas of a day to take on.

Open When You Need A Friend

(inspired by the prompt
'open when you need a friend')

As I write this, I find myself wondering where you are at right now; what kind of day has it been for you, is it just beginning or is it coming to an end? I wonder what a day in life looks like where this letter finds you. I wonder where life has taken you and how you've come to be where you are now. Moreover, I find myself wondering what it is about this moment that is making you feel like you need a friend alongside you. Whatever the answers may be, *I am here*. You may be thinking that I am a stranger, too distant to be considered a friend right now. That being said, as of now, I consider myself a friend alongside you.

Friendship can be defined as lasting affection. Despite never having met you, in this moment I love you and have since I began gathering prompts. These letters connect us in a way that invites the essence of friendship. With each letter, I feel we know one another better – the vulnerability on both sides facilitates a small window into the lives of each other.

You are strong, you are known,
   you are seen, and you are loved.
You are cherished, you are worthy,
   and there is so much more in you than you know.

I know it can be hard to accept these truths, but can I share something with you? I will hold them alongside you until you're ready to hold them for yourself. These words of kindness are words I have found myself wanting to hear myself at times from a friend. When your brain tries to deceive you, come back to this letter and remind yourself of what I know to be true.

*Dear friend, **I am here**.*

Open When You're in a Season of Waiting

(Inspired by the prompt
'open when you're in a season of waiting')

To wait is to stay and hold out until the time is right.
How do we *know* when the time is right?
The truth is, often we don't.

To wait might appear to be a test of patience and endurance, but what if our season of waiting was really a season of preparation? Is it possible that we spend so much time holding out for what will happen next that we forget to take the opportunity to allow this season to be a gift?

What if we camped out and allowed ourselves to wait without the weight of expectation? Would the burden be lighter, and could our hearts be steadied by a period of waiting that allows us to be… still hope-filled and alive to possibility but at peace in uncertainty? It is okay to wait and not know exactly what you are waiting for or how things will turn out. While the world might tell us otherwise, this time and space is for you as you are… hold out until the time is right. Exist moment by moment until you feel ready to take on whatever you find you're waiting for – that way, a season of waiting is gifted to you rather than imposed upon you.

Open When Hope Feels Lost

(inspired by the prompt
'open when hope feels lost')

There is always that moment in a fictional story where there is a push and pull between one decision and another. The protagonist could either be defeated or advance on and be a hero. It's the turning point where things could go either way, but the audience anticipates that all will be well in the end.

In the films, this moment is heightened with an epic soundtrack that radiates hope for us. I think of the moment when Aslan arrives on the battlefield towards the end of *'The Lion, The Witch and The Wardrobe'*. In reality, hope can be harder to find at times – the addition of a world-renowned film score would make all the difference!

When hope feels lost, it can be daunting to know where to begin looking for it. You might not even realise its absence until it has, at last, found its way back to you. The scary reality of the dark places that our brains take us to is that there are instances where hope might seem lost entirely. I have been there and still find myself in the grips of hopelessness from time to time.

However, in these moments, those who love me, know me, and care for me never give up on holding out hope for the promise in my life – even when my hope appears to falter. Even when it is hard to accept their belief in me, I must allow lightness in so that my story can be upheld by hope. I appreciate that not everyone will feel that they have people around them who are rooting for them, or you may believe that people are believing in a lost cause, but I want you to know that I am believing in a story of hope for you – truly.

Personally, I find comfort in knowing that we walk among others who have believed that the signs of hope had faded, yet they planted their faith in the unknown and trusted that a whisper of possibility could overrule the deafening pull towards a heartache that is too huge for some to bear.

I have been moved by many stories of hope, including those shared with me through writing this book, and I have been inspired to look at my circumstances with as much hope as I can muster. Though our stories are unique, the sensation of hope is universal and embedded within us (even when it feels as though it is buried deep beneath the surface).

For everything that is yet to make sense, may you know that hope is never lost! Though we may never come to fully understand why things happen the way that they do, and while this season may feel impossible, your story is far from over, and there is every chance that things can be better than they are right now. I trust that hope can be restored and lightness can be found in the most unlikely of places, and I know that you are worthy of blooming in the light of hope.

Open When You Feel Happy

(inspired by the prompt
'open when you feel happy')

If the word 'happy' doesn't immediately remind you of yellow minions in blue dungarees or an iHeartRadio playlist, then it is possible that you missed out on the whole era that was 2013. Everywhere I went, this song followed me: every car journey, dance class, and assembly hall. My brother recalled once that the song reminded him of his morning paper round for the same reason - music-making genius but this song is the definition of an earworm! That being said, it is the kind of song with the potential to lift the mood of any space, and I loved it for that. Part of the beauty of this song was found in witnessing the joy that others would experience when they heard the modern Motown opening. Like happiness itself, this song had the power to change an atmosphere – a total crowd-pleaser for this generation.

I find myself smiling while writing this letter. When I imagine you smiling or sitting within the warmth of happiness, I can't help but feed from your joy! Happiness is one of those feelings that glows in ways that it is hard to describe. Thinking about happiness takes me back to moments like our leavers' drinks at the end of sixth form, watching my siblings make strides forward in uncovering who they are, hearing my mum sing like nobody is listening, or witnessing love shared between friends, family, and strangers. Happiness beams a certain lightness with a gentle touch that creates a distinctive weightlessness to all that is around. My heart is full knowing you'll be radiating wherever you are (happiness must be one of the most infectious gifts from life itself).

Dear reader, soak up this feeling - absorb it. Try not to fret over how long it might stick around or question where it has come from. Treasure its joyous, yet comforting, touch and carry it with you like an audible ray of sunshine in your pocket.

Chapter Nine | Letters from Nature (Part II)

Cumulous, Stratus, Cirrus

(inspired by the prompt
'clouds')

My papa taught me many things, things like how to keep a logbook, check my car mileage, and how to work through a Sudoku puzzle in record time. Along with these noteworthy life lessons, I learned from him in less obvious ways too. I could see how he observed the world and was a part of it. Papa would often make a point of observing the sky, encouraging me to turn my attention towards the clouds. I always admired the way that he could identify the cloud types but also the stories he told with them – teaching me more about myself. Papa encouraged me to see that the clouds told a much broader story than would first appear. Though I have a hazy recollection of the cloud formations, this prompt reminded me that clouds can reflect a sense of fullness and belonging. What I have come to realise is that we are a fragment of something special – whole in our own right but also part of something bigger.

They ask me if it is lonely to live with my head amongst the clouds; it isn't. Amongst the clouds, I feel weightlessly grounded – each part of me welcomed home. The stories written in the clouds remind me that I am, in fact, not alone – ever.

At times, I am Cumulus, childlike and naïve. I can be sure of who I am, and I can relish being one of many perfectly formed clouds. On occasion, I am Stratus, or perhaps Nimbus – grey and low hanging in the sky. Though the heaviness weighs down on me, eventually we rain collectively. As Cirrus, I can be wispy and wild in all the best ways. I can dance upon the sky's stage and embrace imperfection at its finest.

Where My Feet Wander

(inspired by the prompt
'describe your favourite holiday location')

Upon thinking of the roads that I have walked, my senses are awakened. I can place thoughts and feelings along the paths that I have wandered and recall memories of who I was, but more so than that, I can reflect on what these places have meant to me and see their long-term impact on my life.

Often my favourite holidays have been associated with a sense of belonging or making a 'home' wherever I could find it, even if *my* place there was temporary. Each location holds a special place in my heart making it hard to choose a favourite as such, but I'd love to share with you some of the moments that I have experienced while my feet have wandered.

The Cornish Shores

Cornwall remains a firm favourite, the destination for many of my childhood holidays, a sanctuary in times of need, and a backdrop for precious moments of both solitude and family. I have spent countless hours jumping the waves of the Cornish shores with some of my favourite people, and by the age of eighteen, I reckon I had become a connoisseur of cream teas across countless Cornish towns. Polzeath, a small village located around six miles from Wadebridge and a renowned surfing hotspot, has become like a second home to me.

In the early days of family holidays, each year we would arrive in our blue campervan and set ourselves up for two weeks in the summer. Since then, I have explored this small section of coastline perhaps more than most do in a lifetime. I have left no path untraced and no ice cream flavour untested! I feel most alive when my feet return to where the waves kiss the sand. My toes test the water and dream bigger and bolder than ever before.

On numerous occasions, I have made my way back to Polzeath, seeking a sense of something that I cannot name. Often, I leave Polzeath feeling more whole than when I arrived. If you have never felt inclined to explore the Cornish shores, may this letter be a sign to find your way there for the first time. I can assure you that you will want to return time and time again. I, for one, am already looking forward to the next time that I find my way 'home'.

Not Quite Highland Scotland

To this day, Scotland is the farthest north that I have ever ventured. The trip was short and sweet, but I can tell you that it didn't disappoint. My gran and I travelled up the west coast of Scotland – stopping off in Glasgow, Loch Lomond, and Largs (the surrounding areas where my gran had grown up).

Hearing my gran tell stories from her childhood was perhaps my favourite thing about travelling with her. We have always had a close bond, but somehow I felt that I could see her more completely. I cannot even begin to tell you how special it was to explore somewhere that was so important to her.

Loch Lomond was like nowhere I'd ever been before. I felt as if I had travelled abroad (exacerbated by a thirty-degree heatwave). The water was clear, the air was still, and with that came an indescribable sense of peace. The forestry around us appeared to watch on as I dipped my feet in the shallows and allowed them to dry in the warmth of the afternoon sun. On our way out of Loch Lomond, we spent a 'wee' while in a local shop that appeared to sell everything, including the infamous MacPherson family tartan.

My family history showed its Scottish roots, and this defined 'home' to me in a new way entirely. I was overjoyed to experience an unmistakable sense of belonging – even on this brief Scottish holiday.

European Adventures

Disneyland Paris stole my heart as a five-year-old girl who just wanted to see the magic in every moment. I thoroughly enjoyed endless croissants and freshly baked bread rolls. (I hope to return to France one day with a newfound love for more adventurous food!) Having had to grow up quickly around the time of my parents' separation nearly three years before, arriving in Disneyland was a reminder to seize childlike joy wherever it found me. Seeing the pink castle for the first time, eyes wide and heart open, was a moment in time that I will never forget. There is no doubt in my mind that childlike joy will be waiting for me upon my return.

Belgium has been my favourite European country since I first stepped foot there on a school 'music tour' in 2014. Despite experiencing some pretty intense anxiety at this stage in my life, I have never felt freer than I did on a bike ride along the river in the city. The roads were flat and easy, allowing my mind to wander and giving me space for the bike to find its way. For a long while after this trip, I had dreams of living in Belgium. I admired the slower pace of living, as well as the sense of space. Perhaps this made Belgium the perfect holiday destination… for there I could find a true sense of escapism.

Home

My feet have wandered to some exceptional places. It would seem my heart has too. Finding and discovering places to call home has been enchanting in every imaginable way. I wonder where your favourite holiday destination or place to visit might be? Dear reader, I hope that your feet wander to places where your soul finds what it most needs and desires. What has stood out to me about my favourite holiday destinations is that they have taken me as I am and allowed me to find what I needed most in each moment. The same can be true for you when you open yourself up to the possibility of finding settlement upon the paths your feet wander.

If You Could See You Now

(inspired by the prompt
'a letter to the caterpillar from the butterfly')

Nothing illustrates the beauty of change better than the caterpillar and the butterfly. Change can be a timely reminder that you are ready for something new. It may require courage, but there is beauty in that too. The metamorphosis may not be straightforward but have patience and wait expectantly…

Dear caterpillar, though you may not see yourself in me, I was once like you are now. There is beauty in you, even when you doubt this to be true. At times, I doubt it for myself, too, despite having already experienced the same transformation that you will. Trust that you will take flight just as you are destined to. There were times when I, too, felt small and insignificant, but the truth is little one, you will flourish in time. As you are, I know you to be bold. Refrain from holding back and dare to dream audaciously in this present moment. As you journey through, you will not only learn your strength but of the power of patience.

Others don't always recognise how testing this journey is. They see the before, the after, and the highlight reel, which doesn't reflect the full experience of living. Right now, when others see me, they see outstretched wings and unflinching flight, but there is little acknowledgement of the transformation that has taken place or the struggle of existing between one state and another. Know that I see it; I see the strength in staying the course and the courage in the waiting. Silk will lace you completely as you rest, and you will emerge with the same wholeness but also the new sense of self that you are deserving of.

If you could see yourself now, I suspect that you might be in awe of whom you become. So, take a look at me – if you can love what you see, then trust the process and hold on in there. The growth day to day might appear small, but you are further than you were yesterday, and when the time is right, you will see what I see in you now.

Changing Tides

(inspired by the prompts
'the sea' and 'grace envelopes me as I paddle out')

It is no secret that I have always loved the sea. Anybody who knows me well knows that the sea calls me, grounds me, heals me, and excites me. The sea holds space for the inner child in me, and it is where I feel most at home. My heart seems to sync with the ocean, embracing the natural rhythms of the waves. Somehow, the changing tides find a way to settle my soul like nothing else can. My anxiety dissipates and the overwhelm lifts with every breath of sea air.

As I write this letter, I have made my way to Westward Ho!, a coastal village in North Devon. There is a mound of assorted rocks and pebbles, which is where I sit looking out towards the sea, with the waves creating a soundtrack for me. Coming here today, my heart felt overwhelmed; I like to come down to the sea when I feel this way. A gentle wind blows through, keeping me cool in the heat of the day. The sun is bright, and it is warm on my skin. The scent of fresh doughnuts is faint in the background, and my lips are drying out and taste slightly salty. I watch swimmers, surfers, and sunbathers scatter the beach, but I'm in a bubble of writing and for just a moment the world seems to pause as I trace the outline of my hand…

Overwhelm can be challenging because everyone has a different way of coping. Sometimes those around us might encourage us to move through these feelings quickly. They mean well, but perhaps you don't feel ready to just yet. I like to take time to feel before moving through the overwhelm as I find this allows me to make space for my feelings.

Perhaps you are in a space of overwhelm now. If so, take a minute, pause, and breathe deeply. Take your hand and trace the outline of it with the index finger of the other.

Notice the way the peaks and valleys feel; I like to imagine them like waves. When physically at the seaside, I like to trace in time with the waves as they roll in.

It is tough to hold on for overwhelm to pass. The ebb and flow of the sea remind me that changing seasons are a natural part of life; this sense of overwhelm will ride out on a wave, just as it rode in. Until then, I am here, and we are breathing in sync with the ocean's motion together. The tides will change and the overwhelm will pass sooner than you think.

***

She is infinite blue with depths we can't imagine. Like a sister, she is always there – comforting and consoling. Over underwater mountains and through valleys, she knows no bounds; those salty formless arms welcome us back time and time again.

Grace envelops me as I paddle out, the tender kiss of the sea cleansing my feet; an open invitation to rest amongst the waves. As each wave rolls in, I feel at one with its movements – like it somehow steadies my breath, anchors my soul, and welcomes me home.

As sure as I am that the next wave will come, I, too, am sure of my ability to roll with whatever comes my way – for the ocean is as boundless as the grace that meets me there, and I am free to boldly declare that I am laced with the same infinite grace.

Embracing The Roar Within

(inspired by the prompt
'a letter about having a lion heart')

To be lion-hearted is to see the potential,
  and embrace it fully with a courageous, fighting spirit.
It is a call to be brave, to be bold, and to be fierce,
  all while breathing out love, grace, and humility.
We are loyal protectors,
  and we nurture one another.
Against every trial and tribulation,
  trust your tenacity.
Let your lion heart prevail and come on through.

I was at an event for women called 'Brave Heart' when I first heard the term 'lion-hearted' used to describe a person and their approach to life. I'll admit, I struggled to accept the idea that I could ever be defined as such – so much so that I came to believe that something in me was fundamentally broken.

As a result, I denied that I could ever be associated with having a lion-hearted spirit. After all, I was surrounded by women who appeared to have their lives together. How could I ever compare? It is safe to say that I missed the point entirely.

Despite our pastor speaking clearly on the fact that everyone in that room and beyond could embrace the roar within them, I had major doubts about my identity, and I questioned whether I had the strength to go on. That is why I wanted to use this letter as an opportunity to explore what it is to be lion-hearted (inspired by my experience of finding the roar within me).

At the time of *Braveheart*, I believed that being 'lion-hearted' meant being faultless (despite our pastor's words projecting not just otherwise but the opposite). During this season, anxiety crippled me, I lacked purpose, and I had a heart-breaking reservation about life. Given that I believed being lion-hearted meant being free of fault, it is not surprising that I struggled to see myself as someone worthy.

In fact, at this point, being described as having a lion's heart seemed laughable. Nevertheless, once I hit rock bottom, the only way was up. With the support of a small group at my local church in Liverpool, I began to question those truths I once believed about myself, replacing them with what was true all along.

Despite still wrestling for self-acceptance, my heart is more open than it has ever been before. In my day-to-day comings and goings, I try to see myself the way that others see me. I may not be faultless or fearless, but I am faith-filled. Even in the darkest of shadows, there are glimpses of lightness in me.

I want to encourage you to get to know the roar within you. Acknowledge your strengths and accept your weaknesses so that you may move forwards in any direction that moves you. Your lion heart will become evident, even if you cannot see it in the moment.

The fighting spirit lies in waiting for you to be ready to embrace it wholeheartedly. Approach each day with a determination that cannot be fought against. I know this can be easier said than done. There will be days that you feel small and afraid, but all you need is already within you. We are not called to live perfectly, but we are called to live boldly, and your lion's heart shines through in the big and the small things. Whether your roar shows itself in whispers or wild roars, your lion heart will see you through more than you could ever imagine.

To Blend In Or Stand Out?

(inspired by the prompt
'a letter about blending in')

The relationship that we have with ourselves is an important one – after all, we are the one person that we will walk alongside for our entire lives. Spending time in tangles of self-loathing is (for want of a better way to put it) a waste of potential. I'm not saying this as someone who has loving themselves down to a fine art, but I am saying it as someone who has spent a long while thinking about how to feel self-assured so that I could stand out in a Millie kind of way.

In many ways, we all stand out. For example, though chameleons can camouflage and blend in, their presence is still noted by those who admire what they do – standing out despite blending in. Their incredible ability to camouflage is their defining characteristic – a beautiful quality – enabling the chameleon to survive and thrive in equal measure. Whether you stand out or blend in (and no matter how you do so), you are cherished and celebrated.

I would say that I was a quietly self-assured child. I had doubts just like everyone else, but I wasn't self-conscious; I didn't worry about what other people might think, and I strode around with a subtle confidence that said I knew who I was. I guess at some point, I was taught to believe that standing out would mean standing front and centre, speaking out, or being the best at whatever it is I was trying to prove myself in. Over time, I began to hold back from putting myself out there, determined to take up as little space as possible. That carefree child became someone who took herself so seriously that her confidence dried up, and the thought of standing out was paralysing, leading me to believe that I wasn't worthy. With patience and appreciation for how standing out might look different for me from season to season, I am learning how to come into my own again.

Whether wearing Doc Martens with dresses in the fall or anonymously leaving letters around my local town to speak kind words to the people of Devon on unkind days, my light is beginning to pave its way. My uniqueness is appreciated by those who know and cherish me, and they love to see moments where I boldly showcase myself in ways that I couldn't before. I know that my family have relished in my ability to be more playful, a seemingly quiet way of standing out but something that I have not always been able to do. Before, the thought of picking on my insecurities publicly was deeply humiliating (even if just between me and someone else). This created a strive for perfectionism, setting an unattainable bar to reach across every aspect of my life. Shortcomings felt shameful, and the human act of making a mistake felt unthinkable.

My brother and his partner taught me so much about how to laugh with myself and embrace my identity in its full glory, whether standing out or blending it. I also surrounded myself with friends who taught me so much about the way they stepped into their own light (without even realising they were doing it). Jenny, Yasmin, Kaitlin, and Jack each showed me in their unique ways that it was okay to be authentically myself. There was so much joy to be found in this embraced humility; a freedom that I had not appreciated could save me.

I want to remind you that you don't need to have it all figured out to embrace standing out. The chameleon's blending defence was also the secret weapon that has given it a reputation to be in awe of. You need not feel torn between the light and the shadow, for you have a unique glow all your own. Your individuality deserves its place, even in soft and delicate ways, and this can be loved by you and by those who love you. Standing out, I have come to realise, isn't about making yourself seen over somebody else but instead about embracing the individuality in every one of us and living authentically in that light. Dare to take up space; allow yourself to be seen as you are. You are worthy – no matter if you stand boldly in the limelight or you radiate from the shadows. Living your quiet, audacious truth is an admirable way to stand out.

Sky Full Of Stars

(inspired by the prompt
'the stars')

Stars play,
inviting the soul to take flight amongst them.
Constellations form,
crafting a map by which to follow.

I will never forget the first time I stopped and looked up at the stars. It was a clear evening in Polzeath, a small town on the Cornish coast. Walking alongside my uncle Tim, we paused for a moment after crossing the bridge over the stream.

He looked up and pointed so my gaze followed his arm to the sky. He drew the lines between the stars, mapping out a formation, the plough perhaps, though I forget now. I was dazzled by the abundance of stars. The formation seemed unimportant for I was far more enchanted with the stories he narrated with the stars…

They twinkle against the backdrop of velvet black.

You may think, why mention the sky when there are balletic stars taking centre stage? I say in response, were the stars not embedded into the night sky, would you be able to see them?

They find their place on the sky's canvas,
brought together by their artist.

There is a fullness in the image of a night sky, a comfort in knowing that each part forms this picture-perfect display. The night sky illustrates that you cannot have stars without darkness.

Dear reader, life is like the stars and sky – choose to see the sky full of stars and see the beauty in the constellations that form. No sky is too black that the stars cannot shine upon it.

Chapter Ten | Looking Up and Looking On

In the Perfectly Ordinary

(inspired by the prompt
'there's beauty in even the smallest of things')

Sleep-filled eyes, sunrise glow,
    water trickling down the shower screen.
A little toothpaste around your mouth,
    the ringlet of hair that falls wherever it wants to.

Zoe Ball's Breakfast Show,
    soft murmuring over the stereo.
The splash of the milk and the clink of a spoon,
    'Have a good day,' we call out to one another.

New melodies to hear,
    and kindness to leave.
Sparks of inspiration to catch with both hands,
    but subtle charm also in the perfectly ordinary.

Starlings gliding in their dozens,
    driving home with the warming radiance of the sunset.
Offering exchanges of the day's peaks and valleys,
    making dinner with whatever can be found in the fridge.

Cosy evening lighting.
    Nighttime Wordle, TV episode, or cup of tea.
Pulling back bed covers, shuffling in,
    nestling your face in the pillow before resting your eyes.

The tender smile at the end of the day that says,
    'Today was a good day'.
The gentle sigh that affirms,
    'Tomorrow I will try again,
    but still, beauty could be found in today'.

Put Your Bags Down

(inspired by the prompt
'leaving things in the past')

There is no denying that everybody has a past. We are each an accumulation of the things that we have experienced – both the positive and the negative – some of which we choose to hold on to long after the fact. As much as our memories provide us with a sense of self that is hard to refute (in addition to being an essential part of living), there are times when our memories from the past might feel as though they do not serve us well. When painful retentions feel as tangible as the day that they happened, that is when we begin to carry a weight that we were never meant to shoulder, least of all, shoulder alone.

I don't know where or when this letter might find you, but I do know that the world has felt pretty heavy lately. As much as some of our experiences have been universal, we have also each continued to carry personal baggage day to day. The bags themselves differ from one another, and we carry the weight of them differently too. Whatever you're carrying today, this letter is an invitation to put your bags down for a moment with me.

Beloved reader, I hear you saying that the bags that you carry are heavy; the heaviness has been building for some time leaving you feeling unbalanced by the weight of the past. Though I know you cannot change the path of your past, I hope that you can acknowledge the strength you've shown, even in subtle ways. Each lived moment is another reflection of your courage. Strength is shown in more ways than one, and you my friend are stronger than you know yourself to be. You are free in this moment to put your bags down; you can choose to allow the weightlessness of peace in. It may feel daunting, perhaps even like a vulnerable decision, to drop the walls that you have built around yourself; however, your past does not deserve the power to rob you of this present moment. You're worthy of rest and deserving of the freedom that comes when you ease away from what was.

Light in the Darkness

(inspired by the prompt 'light in the darkness/hope')

There aren't many moments that render me speechless, but the arrival of a winter solstice sunrise found a way to put me at a loss for words. Who knew that there could be so much found in the commute on an early December morning? I immediately thought of this letter prompt ('light in the darkness'), and I knew that I wanted to articulate the experience here. So, I recorded a voice note as I drove so that I could retell the experience for you.

Tuesday 21st December 2021

There are no words to describe what I am sensing – but I find that I want to try. While driving this morning, my soul felt tired. My hands rested on the steering wheel, and the music echoed over the stereo around my empty shell. My mind rambled, rattling off the never-ending list of tasks unfinished and life untouched, while my body remained still, tame in the unrest.

But, as I drove, something shifted. It took a while to pinpoint, but the energy was new. The darkness lifted, a soft sunrise glow emerging from the east with tones of orange easing on in. I dared not take my eyes off the road, so instead, I admired the fullness of the sunrise from its tender warmth – trusting that the sunrise was out in full glory. Such boldness in beauty, subtleness in grace, and joy in its unexpected arrival.

Wretchedly, a sinking feeling, heavy in my chest, returned as I turned west… that was until I checked my review mirror. Now, I can see the sunrise behind me. The clouds have a newfound lightness, puffed up in rosy copper skies. Looking back, I can see the light through the darkness, and looking forward, I can feel the hopeful warmth stretch across my back.

Even on the darkest day of the year, the light has found its way to me. I will be okay, for the light will always find its time to surface amongst the dark.

For When It's Time to Let Go

(inspired by the prompt
'a letter for when it's time to let go')

Life calls us into a variety of relationships: with family, friends, significant others, colleagues, and even perfect strangers. We spend so much time in the company of others that it is understandable that when some of these relationships inevitably change, we can be left with a whole range of feelings. Sometimes letting go can be freeing, but it is challenging when letting go involves feeling a change in you. Dear reader, I hear the grief in the retelling of what was, and I see the courage it has taken to say that you feel it is time to let go. You can feel saddened by this change and still permit yourself to let go of what you need to. Grace will lace every moment that falls upon you, and, with time, you will find the peace within yourself.

I've found myself thinking about times when I've had to or chosen to let go. I think one of the hardest was trying to rediscover who I was. When I lost certain friendships or relationships, it was easy to lose a sense of self with them. Whether it was my zest for life when I experienced relational breakdowns or my soft-heartedness when I was bullied in high school, letting go made it feel as though I'd given up or like there was something wrong with me. I believed that who I was could no longer be – that there would be pieces of me missing forever. We don't always talk about the pain of letting go, but perhaps maybe now is the time to open ourselves up to talking about the experience and just how we might navigate the thoughts that come.

I want to remind you that though relationships may change and shape us, they do not define us – regardless of their relationship with you. I wish I could go back and tell sixteen-year-old Millie this. People grow and change, but we are all an accumulation of life's challenges, the experiences and feelings we've had, and the love that was shared.

We gather pieces of ourselves along the way, some are definitive while others are merely part of the overall puzzle, but whatever brokenness you are healing from, you are still capable of reaching a point of feeling whole.

As much as letting go can be painful, it can also be freeing. Despite there being times when letting go was excruciating for me, somewhere beyond that was always indescribable freedom, even if that feeling was challenging to come to terms with. I'd encourage you to give yourself the same grace that you so freely extend to others. There may be times that you feel you are through the toughest moments, and then something else rocks the boat and you feel like you never come through. When that happens, remind yourself of how far you have come.

Letting go is not a definition of your life
but a shaping of your circumstances.
There is beauty to be found in a change of path
that may lead you where you need to be.

When the freedom of it all seems a distant promise,
trust the process.
Even in spaces where you feel
letting go has left you missing a piece of yourself,
you are whole.

You are loved, and you are worthy of such love –
just as you were, are, and ever will be...

The Beacon on the Rock

(inspired by the prompt 'lighthouses and hope')

Lighthouses speak in beams – brightly and broadly reaching out into every kind of darkness. Their light reaches out as far as can be seen, a beating heart throughout it all, remaining steadfast and enduring in the toughest elements.

Though their paint weathers, the lighthouse's stance is firm; it never wavers, not for a moment. When the seas are choppy and there are rocks ahead, the beams reach out to illuminate a safer path. At the point of no return, when hope seems to falter, the flashlight seeks out the lost and the lonely – bringing them home.

Chapter Eleven | Written In Colour

Feeling Red

(inspired by the prompt
'an expression of the colour red')

With many interpretations of the colours around us and thousands of emotions to pick up on in the colours that we see, how beautiful is it that we get to find meaning within life's paint palettes? With that in mind, I find myself curious about how you see colour in what you see and feel…

What is the colour red?
When I see red, my mind wanders between life's intense emotions, more so than when I reflect on other colours. Sure, I see ladybirds in flight, crunchy apples, and ruby slippers, but ultimately, I feel more. Red reminds me of the best and worst of what we can feel as individuals who experience the world, so I am led to explore the colour red in terms of various feelings.

Love
Both the heart and the home – I ask that love has no choice but to find its way to you. You are worthy of love in the depth of the unknown; let it fill you and let it overflow. Of all the things that there could never be too much of, love is by far the one that appears to do the most good.

The intensity of love is what allows it to live and breathe – existing in even the most trying of circumstances – its depth beyond what we could even imagine.

Sacrifice
Poppies are a masterpiece of nature; we've seen them grow even in seemingly hopeless terrain. A casual beauty, and subtly proud, flushed petals flourish in the prime of spring into summer. They catch the breeze in their flower heads – soaking up the rays of the sun. There is such poignance in their tender growth, a reminder of sacrifice, yet a renewal of hope.

Anger
Anger is a sensation that many of us experience, yet so few of us know where to place it; it burns within harsh whispers, scorching even in places where it does not belong. Dear reader, you are allowed to feel the things that anger you. At one time or another, you may have learned that it wasn't safe to express such a strong emotion, but it is there for a reason. Don't be afraid to be curious about it; question it and study it if needs be. We feel for a purpose that goes further than we can reason out or explain.

With anger comes change, revolution, and a righteous sense of the injustices of the world. So, find safe spaces to feel your feelings. When you do, I hope that you are met with the gentle response that you deserve and that you can grant yourself grace along the way as you navigate your emotions to their full potential.

Embarrassment
With flushed red cheeks and an ache in your stomach, embarrassment can be paralysing, but you don't need to be afraid of it. The dance of self-sabotage in the form of embarrassment will hold you captive in a reflection of yourself that may not be true. With feelings of embarrassment comes a prompt to laugh with yourself and to embrace what it is to be human. Dear reader, surround yourself with loved ones who show you the joy in learning to celebrate imperfection and all its joyous complicated companions.

Passion
What would we be without passion? Without passion, we might fail to show compassion and humanity, and we might cease to show the true value that we place on the things that matter to us. To be passionless might leave you feeling lifeless; allow yourself to feel deeply in oh so many ways. Let passion fuel your dreams and fire up your life in unexpected, meaningful ways.

Tiny Fires

(inspired by the prompt 'orange flames')

I remember sitting alone once (bear with me, it gets better) in a pub (better already!) with some time to spare before meeting some old school friends. This rare opportunity to spend some time doing nothing was a little daunting but enchanting. Despite bringing a fresh copy of Delia Owen's *'Where The Crawdads Sing'* to read, I simply sat at the table in the pub and let the world pass me by. As the evening fell upon the pub, someone came round lighting wine bottle candles. Her eyes caught my distant gaze. She smiled at me kindly as if aware that I was somewhere else. The reflection of the dainty flame grabbed my attention away entirely.

The candle flame flickered in the window against the backdrop of dusk, its movements subtle but darting with elegance. The haze around it made it seem like it was dancing upon the candle stick, the wick a pointe shoe where the lines could blaze with intent. Before I knew it, the hour had passed and my friends arrived. The twinkle of the candle appeared to be a long-lost moment of serenity… that is, you see, until now.

In the notes section of my phone that evening, I wrote a few words, ones that appeared to be on my heart. To be honest, I forgot about it until this letter prompt came through, so I believe that they have been lying in wait for a moment such as this – perhaps waiting for you.

I wrote,

'Let tiny fires trailblaze the way for you.
Admire their ferocity
and be in awe of the flames' audacity to glow.
Allow your heart to remain soft;
this season may have reduced you to embers,
but the fire in you cannot be stomped out.
No matter what tries to consume that bold and beautiful spark, you will shine on."

A Yellow Tinge Of Friendship

(inspired by the prompt
'yellow')

If you'd told sixteen-year-old Millie that she would one day be surrounded by the yellow tinges of friendship, she'd never have believed you. With confidence at rock bottom, many of my 'secure' friendships robbed from me, and a seemingly endless stream of rejection flowing through my life, I was certain I would never feel close to those I did life with again. All of that changed beyond my wildest dreams, and now I find that my friendships are filled with a richness that I could have only dreamed of as a teen. I could list a thousand ways that friendship has made itself known to me since the day I thought the lightness had gone; it has become a listless joy – yet somehow, I still want to share this image of friendship with you…

I find that a yellow tinge of friendship glowed in someone who came into my life by accident yet has remained in my life with purpose. It laced itself within a conversation on a bench on my first day in sixth form. Friendship found its way onto the soles of my dance shoes at seventeen, the laces of petrol-blue Doc Martens at eighteen, and black Wellington boots at twenty-two. It paved its way on countless road trips and meandered around Liverpool, as well as hours upon hours at the theatre. That yellow tinge breathed energy through car breakdowns, cake baking, and time shared at the aquarium watching the rays while linking pinkie fingers. With golden understanding, mellow empathy, bold bright hope, and restorative kindness, the yellow tinge of friendship has enabled me to flourish into the woman I am today.

The 'yellow' in your life is the one who makes it feel like you are returning home – the one who knows you profoundly. Your 'yellow' is your soul person; they are a moment in time that you will never be able to forget because of the way that they made you feel. I hope that you know a yellow tinge of friendship, and if not, I hope that you find it with me.

Through the Lens of Green

(inspired by the prompt
'the colour, green')

A sense of renewal, a reassurance against the fragility of life – focusing instead on its boldness and its beauty. Abundant blessings, crisp dew drops, and the resounding of new life.

The colour green reminds me of spring. I adore the arrival of this season because the world appears to relish in its awakening. There is something special about seeing the world shift throughout the seasons, modelling the beauty that can be found as life changes around us.

Anybody who knows me will know that I have loved farm animals since I was tiny (as a child, piglets were my favourite). There is a particular photo of me at three years old on a day trip during the spring to Cotswold Farm Park. My hair is in plaits, and I am wearing a blue sweater and red Wellington boots, alongside the broadest grin. I spent the day in my element, and since then, green has always reminded me of the fullness found in new life. Funnily enough, I found similar joy when helping out at a local farm during lambing season in 2020.

The smell of fresh rain and the mud in the green fields made the barn feel cosy. I treasured this experience, not only because the lambs were super cute but because I felt more alive than I had felt in months. Somehow, arriving at the farm felt like arriving home, and I left renewed. This same feeling appeared when feeding local calves with our family friend Pip.

There is a youthfulness found in the hues of green, a sense of energy that can't always be found elsewhere. Those days spent watching the farmyard animals have remained with me for life, not only for being wonderful experiences but because of the way the colours around me and the moments created made me feel. Embrace the renewal in the tinges of green and seek to cherish watching life emerge at its fullest; I promise you that you won't regret it.

The Colour Purple

(inspired by the prompt
'a list of purple things – my favourite colour')

Purple Onion
Kale and Cabbage
Aubergine and Purple Grapes

Cadbury's Chocolate
Blackcurrant Jelly,
perfectly set on a China plate

Lilac Flowers
Violets and Lavender
Iridescent Purple Backed Starlings

Emperor Butterflies
Amethyst Stone
Prince's 'Purple Rain'

The Cheshire Cat
Rapunzel's Dress
A Purple Cloak with Golden Stars

Royalty, Nobility, Ambition, and Power
Creativity, Mystery,
and Magic

Rainbow Connection

(in response to the prompt 'rainbows')

Dear reader, you know as well as I do that some things in life cannot be captured by words in the same way that they can be captured by the eye or the heart. Some things are just too beautiful to be viewed second-hand, and some experiences seem to transcend what can be expressed or created. Rainbows, it would seem, are one of those things.

I believe rainbows are pretty special. Some say that rainbows are merely an optical illusion, and sure, they're right. Deep down, I know that rainbows aren't magical, but to me, they feel beyond the realm of reality. The unique blend of technicolour fills me with a sense of something that I don't quite understand. I wish I could bottle up the feeling of a rainbow connection and share it with you, but the best I can do is to try and describe it through this letter.

I wish I could remember seeing a rainbow for the first time. I don't know where or when rainbows took on such meaning or why they became important to me, but they did seem to become significant in my life at one point or another. What I do know is that in moments of desperation, I would find myself holding my breath, waiting for one to appear. Rainbows became something I longed for and something that I chased after.

Whenever hope seemed a little lost and the skies looked greyer than before, rainbows would form glorious coloured arcs across the sky. When peace seemed furthest from my grip, they'd find a way to make me think a little less and breathe a little deeper. When I needed to trust in the promise of hope, there they would be, waiting for me. They'd find their way to the sky's canvas and something in me would feel restored.

I found the year of my twentieth birthday particularly difficult; it was like the world was only available to me in shades of grey. That being said, I went down to Crosby Beach with my dad on my birthday, and a rainbow appeared while we were there. I felt filled with a sense of promise, albeit for a fleeting moment.

I know that in all likelihood, experiences like this are completely coincidental, but when all signs of the colour in your life have faded to grey, you catch hold of the signs of promise as tightly as you dare. You clutch to connection with both hands and chase those rainbows with the hope of inhabiting that feeling for as long as you can. I can't promise that you will experience the same relief in the appearance of a rainbow or even that they will appear just at the right time for you. What I can say with certainty is that hope and promise are all around, particularly when you seek them out.

***

26th November 2019 | 14:15

The light reflects and refracts
causing sun-kissed raindrops to glisten and cast colour.
Soft tears wet my face,
but my eyes look up to see what I can only describe as truth.
Hope is here and peace rests upon me.
The chromatogram grows ever bolder,
and the promise of home draws nearer.

***

During this same season in my life, I would play 'Rainbow Connection' through my car stereo on repeat. I love the rendition performed by Sleeping At Last, but I won't judge if you reach for The Muppets.

When I couldn't see the rainbows, I chased them anyway by listening to a song that brought me the peace I desperately longed for. I craved the technicolour arches and the feeling that I couldn't describe. This song brought all of that and more, even without the physical representation of them in the sky.

Chapter Twelve | Fighting Feeling

Feeling Your Feelings

(inspired by the prompt
'feeling your feelings')

Each of us has a different approach to feeling our feelings in order to make our way through our circumstances around us. It's funny, sometimes I think I am good at feeling my feelings, and other times, I am less so! I engage with other people's feelings with ease – give me an episode of NBC's *This Is Us* or a song by Sara Bareilles and I am all up in my feelings. I imminently find myself feeling *their* feelings for them, regardless of whether my story connects with what I'm consuming. However, ask me to sit with *my* feelings and I'm the first to retreat.

What if we could feel unapologetically before we try to control what comes? Would it be such a bad thing to allow our feelings to the surface, exposing parts of ourselves that we seem intent on hiding? Could there be freedom in allowing ourselves to **feel** our feelings…?

Feeling is one of the most natural human experiences there is, but we've learned over time to try and control and edit down the feelings that we experience.

I have been known to push my feelings away without even knowing that I am doing so, or they unexpectedly spill out over a spilt brew or a lost pair of shoes.

Long story short, emotions can be unpredictable; so, allowing space for the illogical nature of our feelings is essential. Even now from time to time, I spend far too long believing that I have to justify my feelings. Sure, it's good to talk about the how and why, but I am learning that the most important thing is to feel the unfiltered reality of what is on your heart and mind.

I have begun to trust that I don't have to be brave all the time. There is beauty in fully feeling the weight of my love, my grief, and my joy, alongside every other feeling that I cannot always name.

Dear reader, acknowledge your feelings when you are ready to. Recognise them and lean into them where it feels okay too. Take *this* moment to notice where you're at today. Ask yourself 'How am I feeling?' and then ask yourself 'How am I *really* feeling?'

If you're anything like me, the answers may often be different – both are valid, but perhaps one is truer than the other. With time, maybe the former will be as authentic as the second time you ask yourself. It is okay for this to take time and practice – it might take checking in with yourself twice. Just know that it is okay to see life through two lenses at once, sometimes even multiple lenses. There is space for your feelings and experiences in all their fullness, a whole depiction of what it truly is to live.

The Olive Branch

(inspired by the prompt 'growing emotionally')

Here but not here, there but not there; a weird middle ground between asleep and awake. An autumnal morning in the forest, the surroundings still yet alive with the sound of birdsong. The light dances between the branches around me, beaming light into the darkened spaces. To my left, a rustle! Leaves fall from the tree, littering the floor, and from them emerges a white dove carrying an olive branch in its beak. I reach out to take it but it's not quite within my reach…

I slowly awakened to the sound of birdsong. A warmth radiated through me, and a vision of the olive branch remained etched in my mind. Keen to feel the air on my face, I wrapped up in my winter coat, fumbled down the stairs, and went to sit on the front doorstep. A robin, small yet spritely for such an hour in the morning, darted over to me, mouth clutching twigs clinging on to the last leaves of the season. He drops one at my feet, not quite an olive branch but a sure sign that I was meant to take it reminding me to allow myself the grace to receive it…

Spilling the Tea on Perfectionism

(inspired by the prompt
'a letter on how to let go of the need to be perfect')

'I just want to be perfect.' I know that these words have tumbled out of my mouth. The truth is that nobody is perfect and that is okay. I am learning to be at peace with this, even when it is hard to accept. Though the pull to be perfect is stronger than I'd like to admit, I hope in spilling the tea on perfectionism, we can see the beauty in being perfectly *imperfect* together.

1. No one sees themselves in perfection. Fact. Insecurity is a universal experience. I know of no one who looks in the mirror each morning and sees the definition of perfection!
2. Perfection is changeable, and that is why it is unattainable. Every day, every week, every month, every year – there are new standards of what it is to be 'perfect'. How often have we altered ourselves from one version of perfection to another only to watch the standards change? Give yourself permission to exist as you are – take up space and be.
3. What we view to be perfect is not based on reality. Our vision of perfection doesn't even really exist. Therefore, we can take the opportunity to *define* perfection.
4. Allow yourself to make peace with the decisions you've made and the person that you are. Chasing perfection is unlikely to make you happy as you will never feel fulfilled or sustained by it. Our shortcomings do not define us, therefore, learn to embrace them.
5. When all is said and done, no one will remember the faults that you see. They won't see your clothing size, academic record, shortcomings, or 'imperfections'. They will remember how you loved, the way you made others feel, and the impact you made in all the small seemingly insignificant ways. Dear reader, please don't allow perfectionism to rob you of the chance of truly living; it is possible to free yourself from the need to be perfect.

A Penny for Your Thoughts

(inspired by the prompt
'feeling overwhelmed')

Towards the end of my degree, I felt like I was existing within a permanent state of chaos. The list of things that I had to do appeared to multiply rapidly with each day that passed, my concerns for the future followed suit, and the backlog of life that I had been putting off continued to build, whether I wanted it to or not. Outwardly, I think I appeared to have it together (my colour-coded spreadsheets and Post-its keeping me in check), but the state of overwhelm was beginning to be evident to me.

Having woken early on this particular Wednesday morning with a heavy heart and busy mind, I decided to take myself out for the day. I knew that I had to push aside any guilt that I felt for not sitting down with my dissertation and just allow myself the time that I needed. One thing that I have learned about overwhelm is that generally it will continue to build unless you allow it space to dissipate.

After pulling on an oversized hoodie, I grabbed my headphones and set off in no particular direction. It was an unusually quiet morning in Liverpool, which only made it easier to meander with little intent. Though I was unsure of where I was going, it seemed that my feet knew where I needed to be, and eventually, I wound up along the waterfront at the Tate Art Gallery. I was glad to find myself surrounded by the finest pieces of art that Liverpool had to offer.

I ambled around the gallery like I had all the time in the world, reading each white placard, and staring into the faces in each art piece. I had been staring at this particular piece for a little while, for the white noise around me was disturbed by the gentlemen next to me.

'A penny for your thoughts?' he said, peering around at me, his face soft and his tone laced with inquisition. Who knew that such a simple phrase could fill the space between us? Instantly we felt connected.

Overwhelm changes the way that we see things – it is like we can only view the world around us with tunnel vision while simultaneously feeling drowned out by everything we see in our periphery. Something about overwhelm makes us feel like we are in survival mode, and I think that is how I felt that morning; everything around me felt like a blur. Immersing myself in art was a wise move, I guess, but it was the interaction with this gentleman that stopped me in my tracks and lifted the weight from my shoulders, albeit for only a moment or two.

It is unlikely that this man will ever know the impact that he had. I doubt he'd remember even taking that opportunity to reach out to me. His life may have gone on unchanged, but his line 'a penny for your thoughts' has become a defining moment in mine.

When you're navigating a season of overwhelm, it is easy to forget that you are part of something bigger. The lovely writer of this prompt indicated that this season of overwhelm had lasted a long time, and they were unsure how they might fight their way through. I think what I've learned from the moment of connection I found that day is that it is necessary to allow others into our overwhelm. We can try to distract ourselves and tell ourselves that it'll be okay, but, in my experience, the overwhelm will either stay and remain the same or grow (neither leaving you the sense of peace that you deserve).

Dear reader, allow others into your overwhelm – reach within and find the courage to say, 'I'm overwhelmed. Can you help?' In exchange, reach out to friends and strangers alike – say, 'I'm here. You are seen and cared for.'

Small talk can make a difference, even if you're not there to witness its impact. In those moments of overwhelm, I hope you are met with an unexpected kindness that breaks through the surface of whatever is taking up space in your mind.

The Strength In Vulnerability

(inspired by the prompt,
'the strength in vulnerability')

There is strength in connecting with others in light of our lived experiences. Even in the darkest parts of who we are and what we've been through, there are still places where the light can reach us. This might be hard to accept, but what if we could see the strength in what it is to be vulnerable with each other in a way that allows our experience of life to be seen without shame?

At times, the beauty of our stories lies in the raw, unfiltered, and sometimes unflattering truth, and I have come to believe that vulnerability enables us to connect and hold space for each other in a unique way. I'm not suggesting that pain or trauma *should* be what binds us. I acknowledge that there are things that happen that one has to bear that should never have been a burden. If that holds true for you, I'm sorry. My heartfelt hope is that you can allow vulnerability to bridge a gap between you and the support waiting for you. What I *am* saying is that the parts of our story that we are reluctant to share, that we try to control, or that feel laced with shame, need not be hidden in plain sight anymore.

I know that there are days when it feels like no one can be on the inside of the loneliness with you. Nobody knows what it is like to be where you have been or can feel the pain of the ongoing mental gymnastics it takes to live out your day-to-day truth. I want you to hear in this moment that I recognise your strength for what it is. I hope that as you allow others in, the isolation will be dissolved by a level of empathy you couldn't have even imagined existed. By acknowledging those places where light is absent, lightness will pave its way into the vulnerable places of your story until you feel it again.

There is no height or depth that you must journey alone. While life brims with joys and pains, it is okay to trust in those around you, to need them, and to believe that better days are ahead.

Come as You Are

(inspired by the prompt 'yesterday')

Do you ever get that sense that you cannot quite escape what has come before? Ironically, this letter follows one about finding strength in vulnerability, for I want to take this moment to be vulnerable for a second. This book was intended to demonstrate how we are all connected by our stories, so I hope that in taking a moment to boldly come as I am, in some way, this letter won't seem like it is written by an outsider looking in.

Yours, Sincerely thus far has shared some of those experiences and nagging thoughts that have pestered me for as long as I can remember. A close run-in with life's finality brought me to writing this book full of the stories of strangers. While I have come so far in my journey, I have never been quite the same. My life radically changed when I survived what I believed would be my final days. After months of preparing myself to leave the world as I had known it for twenty years, there was something odd about threading myself back into the present day. It forced me to live a kind of double life, which made me appreciate the good days but kept me longing for the opportunity to go back and make decisions that, by that point, were out of my hands. Only lately have I begun to accept that I cannot go back and change the way that my brain responded to the overwhelm of life at the time, but what I can do is claim each day that I chance upon

I do not know where you have been, but I do know that there is space for you – all of you – just as you are. Try not to overwhelm yourself with yesterday. You cannot change what is gone, but you can shape what is to come and grant yourself the gracious gift of peace. Regardless of the baggage you carry, come as you are; bring your joy, your sadness, and everything in between. Be messy and be complicated – and then show up anyway!

A True Gift

(inspired by the prompt 'a letter to a therapist')

What a wonderful thing it is that there are people in this world who care so deeply that they would enter into a therapeutic relationship with another. To me, it is beautiful to think that there are individuals who open themselves up to listening to the pieces of us that are buried so deeply. Dare I say, it is extraordinary that there are individuals whom we can share the joys and pains of life with us in a way that is free from judgement and full of empathy. This world is home to a community of people with different titles, labels, and identities, but all allow us to sit, trust, and talk. Then, we can leave – the burden lightened, and our eyes opened to the possibility of hope (admittedly maybe not instantly, but with time).

Dear therapist, I see you. Your generosity and grace do not go unnoticed. I hear the love that goes into this job, but I also appreciate that there are challenges within your role. There may be days when you feel heavy or uncertain, and this is okay. I also wanted to fill this letter with words you can hold closely on difficult days. So, wherever today finds you, allow yourself to be present and lean into the support around you in the same way that you encourage others to lean into you.

1. You are deserving of the same love and care that you so freely give to those you work with.
2. There is beauty in your ability to breathe life into unrealised dreams and unfulfilled potential. Even in the darkness, continue to find the light that glows between the cracks.
3. When burnout shows up, know that you are worthy of rest.
4. Being human is something that unites us, so try not to be afraid of being imperfect.
5. **When you seek out space for your own healing, I hope that you find your peace.**

Layers of Curiosity

(inspired by the prompt
'curiosity')

Curiosity is one of my defining characteristics. I have always been full of questions and inquisitive. That being said, I have come to believe that curiosity can be a strength and a truly beautiful sensitivity to utilise. Curiosity is layered with unique qualities that serve us well if we only know to access it. A curious nature has given me a better understanding of myself, brought me closer to people (whether I knew them or not), and allowed me access to a peace that I struggle to explain.

With this letter, I want to celebrate curiosity by exploring how I've come to embrace it. Dear reader, be curious with me and you'll find the world opens itself up to you in ways that you are yet to imagine...

Was anyone else a curious child? You'd find my nose in everything! Whether out at the beach yearning to know the depth of the sea or heading into the clouds to dream of all that I could not see. I explored everything to its fullest extent and desired to know more about life around me. By nature (and about it), I was curious. I've come to believe that the very best adventures begin at the peak of curiosity.

There is something wondrously childlike about finding the joy in curious exploration – as is made evident when we consider how much more likely it is that a child will boldly step into what is unknown to them as opposed to an adult.

I think that we could learn a lot from the way that children navigate the world. Many times, I have watched from the sidelines as kids have climbed trees higher than I would dare to. Even when they appeared stuck, fear was far from the forefront of their mind. Their ability to place themselves in the world with little hesitance blows me away – their curiosity outweighs any danger they could foresee! Some adults never lose the ability to see the world with curious eyes, while others only uncover just how much of the world is open to them later in life.

I'm not saying that I will become someone who enjoys climbing a tree for fun, but I am saying that perhaps I could allow a curious nature to filter into circumstances that feel uncomfortable, just as I did as a kid – the perfect reminder for why curiosity by nature can be embraced and marvelled at.

It is my understanding that curiosity brings people closer together. The way that we enquire about those around us and connect with people who have similar or differing experiences to our own is what creates the rich tapestry of human relationships. There is also something to be said about the way that curiosity can play a role in our understanding of ourselves. As time has passed, I have had to learn to embrace curiosity to find my way through life. I'm not sure that I had realised that it was curiosity that had kept me going through some of those more challenging seasons that have come my way. A phrase came to me while I was overlooking Jacobs Ladder in Sidmouth in one of those moments, and it became a sort of motto that I began living my life by when my trust in the future appeared to falter. I said to myself,

*'As long as I remain curious,
I will be okay without knowing exactly what comes next…'*

Stay curious! There is something beautiful about curiosity that I find myself in awe of. Curiosity broadens our understanding of the world and deepens relationships in ways we might not otherwise appreciate. It allows us to be heard and understood in a similar way that empathy does, which creates a means by which to relate to each other and develop compassion for ourselves and others, as well as turn out some pretty great stories to tell.

Stay a Little While

(inspired by the prompt
'battling suicidal thoughts')

I find myself wondering where you are right now. Knowing that this letter is the result of a prompt that was written, I hope that this reaches you at the perfect time.

Battling with thoughts of suicide is undoubtedly one of the hardest things to experience. I know that suicide isn't always a choice that is made but instead a breaking point. The courage it takes to stay and wait out these thoughts is unfathomable unless suicide, in one way or another, has had an impact on your life. I am so sorry if grief has left marks on the pages of your story because you, someone you love, or someone you care for found themselves in unimaginable darkness.

I want you to know that there is no shame in talking about suicide here. Sometimes your brain will blur the truth until you cannot know it clearly anymore. Your mind will create falsehoods and insist that you believe them, twisting the way that you see things. This letter is a hard one to write for many reasons, but I'm here and I am listening to you.

I know that this is difficult to believe but the darkness doesn't define you. The light can be just as much a part of you as the shadows that are cast. Although I don't know each moment that brought you into this space, I do know that on the other side of the grief, there is grace, and somewhere beyond that is joy. It might sound naïve, but there is always a hope bigger than we are. After all, this hope is the reason that I wrote this book.

You are *not* a burden. Suicidal thoughts can make you feel like you are, but you are not. I cannot know every moment of your story, but I do know that your life matters, regardless of whether you believe it in this season. I may seem like a distant stranger, but I hope you know, at this moment, how loved you are. You are seen, even when you feel clouded by this darkness, and I hope you feel able to step into the light wherever you can find it.

Stay a little while and imagine this with me.
Imagine the warmth of the sunrise on your face
or picture its reflection in the sea.
Stay for unexpected moments of joy, laughter, and peace.
Stay to give hope a chance to be louder
than the voice that calls you to leave.

Do not trust the way that you view yourself,
or your circumstances,
when your mind is in a turbulent place.
While there is breath in your lungs
and a dream in your heart,
dear reader, it is never too late.

You are not a burden;
your load can be lightened, and there is always hope.

Stay because you are worthy of all the love that life has to offer.
Stay because one more day could make all the difference.
Even now and even here,
it is never too late to stay a little while longer.

Sometimes the darkness doesn't lift right away; sometimes it takes more time than we might like it to, but I hope this letter acts as the torch that shines a light into where you are. This might sound like speaking from a place of not knowing, but I do know – and I know because I stayed.

I was saved so that I could find new dreams that I didn't know existed. I stayed and wrote letters of hope rather than letters that said goodbye. I stayed and shared my story by living boldly in the truth that hope is real and stayed and sought help from someone who came alongside me. I wrote songs, rewatched *Friends*, breathed deeper, loved harder, adventured wider, hugged tighter, and cheered *very* loudly at a long-awaited McFly concert.

I stayed – and deep down, I know it was worth it.

***

After acting on suicidal thoughts in the January of 2020, I didn't know if I could be okay. It feels important to acknowledge that I could not have come through this season on my own. Below are a variety of resources that offer support specifically for those affected by suicide (more resources and information can be found at the back of this book).

You also do not have to travel through this season alone.

There is support available to you,
and you are worthy of support,
even if you don't believe yourself to be.

***

Papyrus
Telephone Number - 0800 068 4141
Text Number - 07860039967
Email - pat@papyrus-uk.org

The Samaritans
Telephone Number – 116 123
By Post – Freepost Samaritans Letters
Email – jo@samaritans.org

CALM (Campaign Against Living Miserably)
Telephone – 0800 58 58 58

Grassroots
'Stay Alive' App

Chapter Thirteen | The Power of Love (Part II)

The Language Of Love

(in response to the prompt,
'how do I show someone that I love them?')

The language of love is extraordinary. Despite changing circumstances, love as a language remains universal. It exists within us and around us, with the power to shape, define, and change us for the better.

When we think of love, it is easy to jump to fantasies of grand gestures – proposals for example. It is possible that we also think only of an intimate love shared within a relationship, whereas, in actuality, the beauty of the language of love lies in the fact that there are so many ways to express it. For me, love shows up in infinite tiny ways each day. It is the breath that I breathe in the morning, it is a quiet smile from a stranger, it is the presence of friendship in my life, and the way that those around me make my light burn brighter. Of course, love can show up in our intentions, but it also weaves itself into the everyday.

This letter prompt called for ways in which we can show someone we love them. The first step is to exist with it! Love is boundless yet so beautifully bounded in goodness at the core.

I've come to understand that acts of love all require an act of giving. Though love is centred around sensing and feeling, the language of love is also about sharing and experiencing. As a result, love might be less about the who, how, where, and when and more about the why so that you can make an active choice to love. Show love in a way that is meaningful to you, even if that is less conventional.

Loving another person is about choosing to not only light up space as one but to burn together as two flames joined together, ignited with passion, trust, compromise, and respect. Love brings out the best in us. What is love without its lasting impact. How do you know that love was there unless we are in some way changed and shaped by it?

I have recently learned so much about the ways that I show love to those around me. It would appear that the way I show love knows no limits and fights to be a part of just about everything that I do. Conventional love languages in many ways aren't broad enough to accommodate more nuanced acts of love, but a knowledge of the language of love is what allows me to show love to those I come across every day. I talk about the 'why' being an important part of *how* to love because although loving without motivation is beautiful and sincere, there is something special about love that is displayed in intentional ways.

Everyone shows love for one another differently (one of many reasons that I have always admired the language of love). As illustrated in this book, I have always been a words person, but I appreciate that there are people close to me who are not. I, therefore, try to be intentional about loving through actions that meet my loved ones where they are.

The language of love is a powerful one; therefore, may this be your reminder to make space for it and actively express it when the opportunity presents itself. Admittedly there are complexities to the human experience that challenge what it is to love, but I like to believe that loving foundations are what we each build our lives on, and therefore, love is present, even in the most difficult surroundings.

Love could change the world, but when we are dealing with something as profound as the language of love, how do we explore and express love while trusting it to reach its full potential? While the answer may not be simple, showing signs of love is something that is ingrained in humankind. The language of love just so happens to seep its way into perfectly commonplace experiences, just as much as grand gestures and general affections. In whatever way that you give and receive love, allow it space to be present.

When Love Takes Over

(inspired by the prompt 'falling in love')

What a gift it is to fall in love. Sometimes it happens slowly, whereas sometimes falling in love seems instant and unstoppable – either way, it's quite the experience. I hope that you open your heart up to falling in love. Let it enrich your being in the way that it was designed to. May you fall in love with who you are, those around you, and with life itself in light of its wild unpredictability and valiant existence.

Eager and free without limits or second guesses. We try to reason out how the water reaches the sea, but the water feels its way there without plotting out its path. Like a river flowing into the crevices that no one can see, love finds its way and paves a gallant passage ahead.

Let Love Be Known

(inspired by the prompt
'coming out')

Just as our differences can cause distance and division, unity can also be found in the things that make us different from one another. There can be many thoughts and feelings around the experience of coming out. Some may find peace in the process of better understanding the pieces of themselves, whereas others may feel a sense of nervousness when talking about their identity or sexuality. Dear reader, know that this letter is one of love and celebration, just as much as it is a call for acceptance. You are cherished just as you are, and you do not have to shoulder the responsibility of this whole movement. I hope love meets you at every point of the challenges that you face.

As I write this letter, I find myself considering some of the questions that you may be considering in this season, including some of the questions I have asked myself. I think before I may have believed that there was a 'right way' to come out and express identity and sexuality. The more I considered the breadth of these kinds of questions, the more I think I understand and appreciate that each person's 'coming out story' will look different.

***

They have their dreams surrounding my life, but I have a thousand questions. Each question leads to another, which leads to several more – like a flower unfolding petal by petal. I find myself wondering, will I find love and what will it look like? Can I embrace it wholeheartedly?

Will others understand? Can I encourage them to understand and is that my responsibility? Will some judge me if I don't display queerness in the way that people expect? Do I have to dress or act a certain way? Am I too much or too little? Am I enough?

Will I be able to stand with my partner publicly while also being at peace? Can I be a person of faith and still live my truth? Will the world be accepting of my aspiration to be a parent?

Can I be unsure? Do I have to be certain before I speak out? Do I have to come out or can I just be? When love is at the centre, surely nothing else matters.

***

I appreciate that not all reading this letter will resonate with the process of questioning their sexuality, and that is okay. This experience is just as valid as wanting to explore the fluidity of one's sexuality. If this is the case for you, I hope that you celebrate your loved ones, as they are, without judgement. Allow space for experiences that are not your own and remain curious and empathic about the journey of people unlike yourself. There is always space for kindness, there is always space for celebration, and there is always space for love.

If this internal questioning *is* a piece of your story, please know you are loved as you are. The world is made infinitely better by you being in it, and I find joy in seeing people being able to live as their authentic and truest selves. I hope you find the courage to live boldly and that this is met with acceptance – but please also remember that you don't owe the world a 'coming out' story.

Individuality is a beautiful thing to celebrate. I want to acknowledge that I know our understanding of identity and sexuality will change and evolve as these letters age. I am grateful for the opportunity to love and be loved without limits and long may that continue regardless of how the experience of 'coming out' looks years from now.

I Hope This Finds You Well

(inspired by the prompt
'to an ex-best friend')

Friends see our biggest losses, our greatest wins, the lightness around us, and the darkness within us. Regardless of the way that a friendship ends, there can be a feeling of loss from both sides. I have been blessed to do life with some incredible people, some of whom I am lucky enough to still call my friends. Although this is true, I have also lost friends along the way under a variety of circumstances.

When we drift away from people we love or when a friendship ends on bad terms, we don't often get the chance to exchange words that reflect how we really feel. Regardless of whether you resonate with being the sender or receiver of the following letter, I hope it facilitates some level of catharsis. You are deserving of peace. I hope that this provides some sense of that.

***

Dear friend, regardless of the circumstances that led us to this place, I hope this finds you well. It has been a while and the distance has caused me pain, but I think of you often. I do the occasional stalk on Instagram and see your highlight reel, but I find myself hoping that the joy is as real as it appears to be.

We shared something once, something unique and special that cannot be replicated or replaced. Love knows no limits, and I believe it can continue to bridge the gap between us.

I hope that today there is something that makes you smile. Your smile used to light up even the darkest of spaces and radiated brighter than you can imagine. When I think of that smile, I think of the joyous moments we shared between us.

Sometimes I look back at old photographs and conversations and wonder how we got here. Then, I take a step back and remind myself to be grateful it happened at all. There is a hole in my life now that you are no longer a part of it, but the impact you made will last forever. Nothing can tarnish the joy that you brought me.

When things get tough, I hope that you are surrounded with love; allow it in. You are worthy of it even when you don't believe yourself to be. I hope that you have the right people around you when the lows come. It was a privilege to be this person at one point in your life. Thank you for trusting me with the depths of your heart and for enabling me to share mine with you. I hope peace surrounds you. I don't know about you, but I've felt a lack of peace ever since we parted ways. This is me acknowledging that it has been challenging, but I wish you the same peace that I long for. Some friendships are for a season, but I will never stop caring for you.

***

I have come to realise, albeit a little later than I would have liked, that some people are in your life for a season. Sometimes you will build a friendship with someone you believe will be with you for your whole story, but really, they are only there for a chapter of it.

It is important to remember that distance is not equivalent to a lack of love. You can choose to see the love that was rather than give in to the bitterness that can become. If you experience these feelings of loss, I hope you know that you're deserving of peace. Allow the warmth of love to remind you that it exists beyond the human bounds we place on it.

Grief & Love

(inspired by the prompt
'a letter on the passing of a loved one')

Just thinking about my papa blowing out his birthday candles brings my own heartbreak to the surface, though my grief is the witness to both the pain and the joy. What a privilege it was to love him but such agony it brought me to lose him. Papa saw me completely, which was a beautiful thing, but his passing left a void. Only now am I starting to trust that his passing doesn't limit the love I can have for him.

Love doesn't promise to come without the pain of loss, but it does seem to mask the fragility of life. Love is the perfect antidote to fear, allowing us to live in the here and now. So, when life inevitably reaches an end, death leaves voids that haven't been imagined to their fullest depth. As painful as it can be, grief bears witness to a love that surpasses the limitations of life.

***

Some may identify with a need to confine grief to an anniversary or certain occasions. We try so hard to box up our grief or to find a way to explain it when it bubbles to the surface. Grief, I find, is much like love – it just is. We cannot control, confine, or limit it; we learn to co-exist with it. Allowing grief to exist seems unnatural to us, for it is painful and raw, but it can also serve as a beautiful reminder of where love was – even love we didn't realise at the time.

You do not have to earn a right to grieve. It shows up without the need for an invitation. No matter the circumstances, your relation to an individual, or the way that they died, allow yourself the space to feel your feelings – even those that you may find challenging to accept. Your grief is valid however it appears. I hope that comfort finds you in those places…

***

When my Papa passed away, it was like he took a piece of me with him. He saw a lightness in me that seemed to vanish when he was no longer sitting in his green armchair. Grief has a way of creating distance between us and the world. It takes an enormous amount of courage to choose to thread yourself back into the fabric of living when life as you knew it might never look the same again. The instinct, I think, when it comes to grief is to bottle it up and remain silent, but being able to share in the experience of grief is what makes it somewhat less lonely. There is always a space to talk about your love, grief, and the navigation between the two. I wish I had the right words to make the pain of grief dissipate a little for you through this moment. I hope that, with time, you manage to embrace life in all its fullness – allowing space for grief with its many faces and room for a new kind of joy.

Drop the weight of expectation and take a breath where you can. Forever is daunting, so maybe it is enough to concern yourself with one moment at a time. When the thought of eternity feels like too much, allow yourself the opportunity to be present and nestle into what you need here.

***

I know that many will be able to identify with what it is to grieve for a loved one; my heart breaks just thinking of the losses that others have experienced in this season. If this letter speaks to you, please consider this letter a virtual hug. I wish I could pour you a brew and chat over our fond memories together. Cruise Bereavement Support is an amazing charity to reach out to if you are looking for support at this time. Just know that even when your grief feels like it has gone unseen or unheard, I see you and I hear you, and I share in this with you.

To Love & Be Loved

(inspired by the prompt
'agape love')

Love is a necessity, making it your birthright to be loved. If today is a day where that feels hard to believe, I want to take a moment to remind you that you were born with the right to be loved.

When it comes to agape, you don't have to mould yourself into worthiness. Love chose you long before time began, and it will choose you beyond the confines of life itself. You can't earn it or deserve it, it is boundless and endless – a non-negotiable birthright, a gift given without a single ounce of reservation. No matter the circumstances or how unworthy you might believe yourself to be, love that just is without rhyme or reason says that you are loved now and forever, just as you deserve to be.

Chapter Fourteen | To A Perfect Stranger

The Legacy of Kindness

(inspired by the prompts 'to the stranger who smiled at me' and 'a letter to the stranger that complimented me on the day I needed it most')

Isn't it amazing how contagious kindness is? One act can transform someone's day and lead to a chain reaction without this ever being the intention. There is a sincerity that comes with smiling at strangers, perhaps because it costs nothing to connect with another person in this way. These connections can be rare, which only makes them all the more special.

I remember a particular day when I was sitting by the Albert Docks in Liverpool. There is often a steady flow of people there, but I knew it would be a quiet enough spot to sit and enjoy reading for a while. It was early July, and the European 2020 Football Tournament was the chatter on everybody's lips. A young lad on a scooter approached me from behind at speed, startling me a little, though I felt pleased to see him. 'Do you want England to win? Do you think they can?!' he shouted at me. Taken aback, I considered being cynical before instead responding, 'Yeah, that would be nice, wouldn't it?' He beamed from ear to ear and scooted off before I could say another word. A woman, presumably his mum, followed behind him. She looked over at me and smiled at me before continuing on her way.

Little moments like this are about connection. I felt like we had shared a flicker of lightness between us, and it left me with a cosy kind of feeling for the rest of the day. For the days that followed, every time I thought about the interaction, I smiled, and I felt compelled to try to connect with each person I passed, having noted how wonderful it felt. Even now, writing this, I'm smiling at just the thought of them. Kindness leaves a legacy and creates these moments every day, though we might not even realise it at the time. We will all have stories like mine, of interactions we've shared with strangers that have fulfilled us in some way.

If you have ever been this stranger leaving a legacy of kindness wherever you go, thank you. It means more than you know and makes far more difference than you might imagine.

These moments of interaction sometimes extend beyond a smile. There is something special about strangers noticing who you are and affirming that even though they do not really know you. Dear stranger, you didn't know how much they needed you to say those kind words, but you said them anyway. A gentle affirmation can go a long way; an unexpected kindness on the day it was craved the most is not something to be taken for granted. They wanted you to know that it blessed them, but they couldn't find the words at the time, so now I have the privilege of extending that thanks to you. That's the thing about forming a connection with strangers, the interactions can be fleeting, but they leave a significant impression on our lives.

Wouldn't the world be a better place if we gave kindness as if it was second nature? What if we loved with intent and made space for the little moments that matter? Somehow a stranger seeing us so completely has more meaning than when our friends or family try to boost us up, probably because the element of surprise leaves a profound impact. In a world where you can leave any kind of legacy, perhaps it is special to leave a legacy that you do not see the impact of. These selfless moments shape individuals who we do not even know the names of. Interaction keeps us grounded and brightens the darkened spaces of our lives.

Dear stranger, thank you for making the instinctive choice to lift others, especially in a world of comparison and distraction – where it is too easy to tear someone else down or to miss the opportunity to build them up. You make the everyday extraordinary just by being, and you trailblaze the way for kindness. Dear reader, I hope you find interactions like this on the days you need them most. May the world be filled with enough strangers like these that you come across someone who meets you where you are – at just the right moment.

I Think I Already Love You

(inspired by the prompt 'a letter to a future partner')

We spend our lives crossing paths with hundreds of others each day and thousands across a lifetime. Whether online or in person, there are copious ways to meet someone new. However, many of us spend time hoping to have a specific encounter with someone in particular, one we have invested time dreaming of and praying for in one way or another for much of our lives. Some of us may define this significant other as a 'soulmate', a term that, at its core, means to be perfectly matched with another. When you are so in tune with someone, I find that you think of them before you ever come to meet them face to face. With this in mind, and inspired by this prompt, I have written a letter to a future partner, posing some all-important questions but also describing in my own words what such love feels like…

***

How is it that we can feel love for somebody that is yet to come into our lives? Where does such love come from, and where does it go? How do we express the love that has nowhere to land? The truth is, I don't know, but I think I already love you. There is something inherently risky about disclosing romantic love to a stranger, as such, at least that is how it feels, but there have been words on my heart since you were a far-off thought. I want to share them with you here.

My love, I aspire to build a life with you that celebrates us as individuals but also as a partnership. I want you to have everything that you've ever dreamed of while weaving my dreams with yours – so that 'yours' and 'mine' become 'ours'. Allow me into your boldest desires and deepest fears, for when we hold them together, we can pave the way no matter what. Your vulnerability is welcomed here – there is beauty in seeing each other so completely.

I think that we should laugh often! When the challenges come, as they inevitably will, I want us to face them together; no 'you' and 'me', instead 'us' and 'we'. We can throw ourselves at the ups and downs and come out on top if we keep the joy. We will pursue joyfulness and come to find it in each other. If there are times when our circumstances do not appear to be joyous, we will seek joy out anyway and remind ourselves that we are blessed to share life.

At times I find myself wondering if I will be enough for you. I look at myself and my story and the doubt creeps in. When I look at my body, I see imperfections, and when I evaluate who I am, I see shortcomings. Despite what we might like to believe, here I want to acknowledge that we are most likely flawed like everybody else. The difference is that we will see such flaws and choose to love anyway.

I hope that we make space for difficult conversations when they arise so that love continues to win against the odds. May we appreciate the art of compromise and the value of trust so that we can protect and honour one another. Partner, I'm optimistic that we will see the best and the worst in each other but keep love central to the foundations by which we walk. Wherever we land, know that there is so much that can be found, restored, and built within love for it is boundless and reckless in all the best ways.

Upon this page, I want to share with you that I love deeply and wholeheartedly. When I utter the words 'I love you', I am vowing to have and to hold you from this day forward; there is no reservation, just love in its truest form. When we come together as one, trust that you have my loyalty, my protection, and my friendship, no matter what comes our way. From love's first kiss to final breath – even beyond the limits of time – I promise myself to you. I anticipate a love story for the ages, and I look forward to writing within the pages with you.

A Thought about Parenthood

(inspired by the prompt
'a letter to the parent who is struggling')

While being a parent can be joyous, parenthood can also be challenging. I imagine enabling another living soul to navigate this crazy life is a responsibility that is hard to prepare for. I was raised by parental figures who embraced me with love and surrounded me with good intentions. Just as this is true, there were also moments when my parents searched for the right things to say and do. However, for all the messiness of life, I knew that infinite love surrounded me. To love is a powerful thing, so allow it to come into its own! Based on my experience of being a daughter, I am thinking ahead to things I would like to remember should I become a mother. Ultimately, remember that you are doing the best you can with what you know now. There are always things to learn, but what a journey you are on - leaning into a community is step one.

From Me to You
1. You're never on your own in this experience. Others have been where you are right now; they are a living and breathing example of how you can come through okay.
2. Keep standing with your arms open unreservedly and wait patiently. One day, your child may just fall inside of them when you least expect it, and you'll be their safe place.
3. Listen, learn, and adapt – parenthood can be a beautifully collaborative experience. Listen intently to your child, learn from other parents, and adapt your parenting through each season of parenthood as you find your way while the world changes.
4. Allow yourself to acknowledge and accept imperfections and shortcomings - we all have them as nobody is perfect. Try to be gracious, to yourself and to those you journey with. Fill your intentions with love, as there will always be places where it can come through.

Let Me Tell You a Secret

(inspired by the prompt
'a letter to your future children')

When this prompt arrived in my inbox, my thoughts turned to the letters that I write specifically for *my* future children. I began writing letters like these when I was in my teens when I was told that the possibility of me conceiving naturally was unlikely (though I still hold out hope for being a mama one day). I found some sense of comfort in knowing that I was filling pages with words that might one day speak into the life of a soul that I already love so deeply.

The maternal instinct in me is strong, so consider this a letter not just to *my* future children but to each of us still searching for a sense of self in who we were as children.

There is every chance you may feel this letter doesn't directly speak to you, but sometimes it's nice to nurture the inner child within us all with words that we may have needed to hear long ago…

***

Hello little one, what a miracle it is that you're here. Your arrival is precious, and my heart sings at the thought of you. You are beautiful in your own right, perfect in every way imaginable, and most importantly, you are loved.

I am praying boldly and fervently that you know of the affection that surrounds you and that you feel worthy of the space you take up. May nothing distort your vision of that truth or keep you from knowing it as surely as I do in this moment.

You have arrived for a time such as this, and for every peak and valley that you experience along the way, you will find me here – rooting for you as your number one cheerleader. Nothing could separate you from me, our stories are entwined by something beyond words.

Throughout your life, I hope that you are blessed with feelings of immense joy. It is a feeling like no other. Relish in those moments, even when they appear to arrive unexpectedly, for even in unprecedented circumstances, joy is within reach if you only look for it. In the twinkle of a plane light pretending it is a star or in witnessing an elderly couple clutch each other's hands in the street, moments of joy exist all around us, and it is okay to take hold of them alongside our own joyous experiences. Joy laces life without discounting that sometimes life isn't always the epitome of joy, so allow yourself to bask in its lightness as it presents itself.

Who knows what life might look like when you take your place in the world. It changes so quickly that it is hard to appreciate just where you might find yourself. Although, I imagine you will come across some of life's common troubles. So, allow me to let you in on a little secret: even now, I don't have it all figured out. The only way I can respond is with grace.

As the sun rises, with the moon following behind, I face the uncertainty with all that I know as I am in that instant. Grace is something that has saved me countless times, without it I wouldn't be where I am or who I am. Regardless of where you believe such grace comes from, I hope it makes itself known to you in the same way.

My darling children, future caretakers of the days gifted to us, world-changers, joy-bringers, and life-givers, give yourself grace. Give yourself grace so freely that it feels like you are giving it to someone else, no matter whether you find yourself in valleys or on mountaintops. Grace will take you to places you couldn't ever have imagined. It'll meet you in the depths that you thought nobody could see and will inch its way through the darkness – until lightless cracks glow golden. You might not see it now but all that you will require is within you or around you; lean into it and you'll pave your own way. Warm wishes and love for the journey ♥

A Letter to My Future Self

(inspired by the prompt
'my future self')

Well, you did it! Innately, I hoped that you would read this one day. How many years have passed? Several I imagine. There will be things that have changed, although I hope that some things have endured the test of time. Whenever this finds you, there is something to be said about perfect timing. May this letter remind you that it is never too late to shape your story…

For the Things That Change
Through all of life's uncertainties, you have made it here (which is a wonderful thing). I find myself wondering how life may have changed or, should I say, how I *hope* they have changed for the better. All those dreams that nagged at you relentlessly, did you pursue them? The peace that you yearned for; did you find it? Did you learn to love your body? I wonder, did you stop running away when people got too close to you? Are you living boldly and fearlessly as you once promised yourself that you would…? If not, why not?! It's never too late to start now!

For the Hope of Remaining the Same
Though I have dreams of there being growth that I am yet to see, I find myself hoping that *some* things have remained the same. Like, do you still wrinkle your nose when you smile or twiddle your hair between your first finger and thumb? Through it all, I hope the essence of who you were still holds true. There is something special about your uniqueness that I wish you'd embraced sooner; how beautiful it is when we accept that uniqueness can be good.

When I think more broadly than that, I'm intrigued by who you are now and what you might find helpful to remember as you grow into this next season of your life.

We have always enjoyed a good list, so here are a few reminders to tuck in your pocket as a reminder of what I had hoped for you...

1. I hope you kept your love of soft cuddly toys. Perhaps you don't need so many these days, but making room for your inner child will never be a waste of space.
2. Do you still see the best in people? I hope that you never lose the joy in choosing to see the potential in those around you, even when life will inevitability show you the best and worst of people. I hope you hold on to the fact that it is possible to hold space for ourselves while refusing to dampen out the lightness in someone else.
3. When the world expects you to know everything, please still ask curious questions. Others might make you believe that being uncertain or 'on the fence' is a bad thing, but it is this uncertainty that allows space for us to grow as life changes around us. Sadly, the ability to adapt is something we appear to lose sight of as we get older. Curiosity about the way others think or the way the world works can never be a bad thing, even if that requires removing prejudices that limit us to one way of thinking; allow yourself out of the binary.
4. If it all falls apart, it will come back together again – even if it does so unexpectedly.
5. No matter who you are now, I hope that you choose to love – always. Surround yourself with family and friends who celebrate you, cherish you, and accept all that you are. Allow love in and give love without reservation – it is a risk worth taking every time.
6. Please, never lose the desire to want to make each day a little brighter for others around you; kindness is not naivety, it is a timeless necessity that genuinely makes the world a better place. Don't limit the kindness that you are willing to put out there and refuse to become short-sighted; audaciously embrace kindness each day.

Chapter Fifteen | The Unwritten Letter

Having waited for prompts to come in for this project, I wound up with ninety-nine letter prompts. I continued to be patient while I held out for the one-hundredth prompt, but eventually, I started to feel a little disheartened. That was until I realised that there just might be a reason why the one-hundredth prompt was missing in action. It suddenly dawned on me that there would be people that wanted to share their hearts in a prompt but didn't feel ready to. Dear reader, if this resonates with you, then please know that this letter is for you.

Whatever circumstances you find yourself in, no matter what is on your heart as you read this, I hope that you feel enveloped in grace in ways you may not have been before. My hope is that we can feel connected through this letter and that you receive my open invitation to reach out (tweet me, write to me, or connect with me however you feel able to). Writing without a prompt feels a little strange, but somehow, I feel this letter has a purpose. I do not know where this finds you, but as the words find their way from my heart onto the page, there is a sense of something building. Writing this letter feels like a breath; I don't know how else to describe it. It is like I want to breathe love between the pages and watch this book come alive in your hands and your heart. I want to gently take your face between both of my hands, as my youngest brother so often does to me, and ensure this letter isn't just read but felt.

The unwritten letter is no more or less important than those inspired by the ninety-nine prompts given to me. It does feel a little different, but my heart feels no less connected to you. I see your darkness and I see the lightness in you. I hear the pain and I hope for joy. I appreciate the faults and flaws, but I do not dwell on them for a second. You are so much more than what you believe yourself to be. Dear reader, your story is still being written. Let today be the day that you choose to step into what it holds for you. There is an unwritten story for you to write – embrace the blank pages and you will find light between the lines in unexpected places.

A Closing Thought

(Trigger Warning – Mention of Suicide)

There were many reasons why I decided to write *Yours, Sincerely*, the first being that I have always been a letter writer. My first letters included funny notes to my parents amongst classic letters for Father Christmas. I found joy in the art of snail mail, left notes of encouragement wherever I could, and embraced the idea that letter writing was unique in connecting people.

Given my love of written words, when I started experiencing suicidal thoughts, it was unsurprising that writing letters to my loved ones was a necessity for me. Not long before my twentieth birthday, I wrote a number of letters to my closest friends and family ahead of acting on those thoughts with the intention of ending my life (this isn't some grand reveal, just the truth). When my life was saved, I'll admit that it took some time to find my way back to feeling like I was part of this world as it moved forwards; living was the one eventuality that I hadn't prepared myself for. However, with support and with hope fighting to override the hopelessness that I was experiencing, I came to a place where I wanted to rediscover my love of letter writing. With that, *Yours, Sincerely* came into fruition – a project that would bring stories together while raising money and awareness for the suicide prevention charity, Papyrus.

Despite thousands of lives being impacted by suicide each year, there was little out there for those who had acted on thoughts of suicide and survived (particularly for young people). I also discovered that the term 'suicide survivor' was attributed to those who had lost loved ones to suicide and that most suicide prevention charities work alongside those who have been bereaved. Despite the undeniable impact of acting on thoughts of suicide for *all* involved, I felt there was a notable gap in support available. While I knew I couldn't shoulder this responsibility alone, I felt driven to make a difference. This book, I hope, is just the start.

I'd like to take a moment to say a few words in reflection …

If you're battling those daily thoughts, I want you to know that you don't have to hold the weight of them alone. Say you're in the process of reaching out for support, hold in there. You are worthy of people's time, knowledge, and love. To those recovering from acting on suicidal thoughts, no matter what took you to that place, I believe that there is a way forwards and an alternative way out. You have known a depth known to few, but your presence on this earth is cherished more than you can imagine. My heart next goes to those who have been bereaved by suicide; I ache for your loved ones just as much as you do in this moment. Life is so beautiful yet so unbearably unjust at times. I hold space for your grief and all the love that it signifies. To those who stand beside others experiencing these turbulent thoughts, your patience and kindness are a comfort, and I thank you. Lastly, to the souls we have lost, to those who couldn't be saved, to the people we know who still had so much life left to live, all I can say is that you matter dearly, and I hope you are free from whatever burdens you carried. While your story is your own, I carry your story with me in my everyday comings and goings.

All that being said, my main reason for writing this book was a necessity to illustrate that life is multifaceted in a way that I hadn't appreciated before now. Dear reader, I hope you leave this book closer to the knowledge that while life can be painful, there is far more beauty to come out of it. Thank you for allowing me to share parts of my story in this space but also for having the courage to meet me here. There is so much I could say, but I only hope that this book speaks for itself. The last thing left to do is to remind you just how loved you are (it can never be said enough). I am so grateful that you chose to pick up my letters.

Yours, Sincerely,
Millie x

Acknowledgements

Yours, Sincerely epitomises the saying 'it takes a village'. I could never have written this book alone. For all the things I have ever been uncertain of, I was never left doubting whether I was loved – even when brain trickery tried to tell me otherwise. I am blessed to have been surrounded by close friends and family (too many to name) as I've undertaken this project. You know who you are, and I thank you.

To those who have encouraged my love of writing and harnessed it into something I could be proud of (Blue Poppy Publishing and Lora Rovena), there aren't words enough to express the gratitude I have for the freedom you've gifted me.

There were many who listened to me when my future seemed bleak, and just as many celebrated my wins. You bought me time so that I could ground myself on firmer foundations in order to write this book and boldly hope for a brighter future.

As I expressed several times within this book, I know that the world will change beyond the words that I have written here. I will learn and grow, but ultimately the vision remains the same. The thing that will not change is my heart for people, no matter how the experience of living fluctuates.

The most important acknowledgement for *Yours, Sincerely* goes to you, the reader, and those individuals who shared prompts with me when this book was in its infancy. You breathed life into my passion project, giving me purpose and providing the framework for love to come pouring out of me. I had so much to give, it was overflowing abundantly, so to have the opportunity to stand with so many others – each of you sharing pieces of yourself with me in unique ways – has been life-changing. I will forever be shaped by the experience of writing this book, so I very much hope that it shapes you too. Love to you all, always.

Who Can I Turn To?

Resources For Those Needing More Right Now

Sometimes, when we become isolated, we find ourselves trying to outrun our feelings or circumstances, but I know from experience that you can't outrun them forever. While I hope that these letters provide some level of escape and comfort, or instil a sense of hope at this time, I feel compelled to offer something beyond what I have written for those needing a little more right now (knowing that life's burdens are heavy to carry alone).

Dear reader, you're *not* alone. Many charities, and resources are available to you – some of which I have listed below should you need them (for yourself or for somebody you know). I cannot tell you exactly what to expect, or how reaching out may impact your story going forward – but I do know that the quickest way to invite another alongside us in our loneliness is by talking about whatever keeps you from the peace you deserve. Before your brain tries you tell you otherwise, you *are* deserving of this and so much more.

PAPYRUS Prevention Of Young Suicide
Website: www.papyrus-uk.org
Telephone Number: 0800 068 4141
Email: pat@papyrus-uk.org
Text Number: 07860 039967

PAPYRUS Prevention of Young Suicide is the UK charity dedicated to the prevention of young suicide. The charity supports individuals under the age of 35 who are experiencing thoughts of suicide, and anyone at any age who is concerned for a young person who may be experiencing thoughts of suicide. Advisors at PAPYRUS can help set up unique safety plans alongside individuals, which can be revisited even after the initial contact has taken place.

HOPELINK is a practical and pragmatic way of keeping a safety plan to hand during those hardest moments.

PAPYRUS's suicide prevention helpline, HOPELINE247, is also able to support professionals as they work alongside young people, or work through their own experiences – working with first responders, doctors, nurses, police officers, counsellors, teachers, and pastoral staff.

In addition to this, PAPYRUS advocate for change in the community – researching how things are changing, sharing their knowledge far and wide, and speaking up for those impacted by suicide.

Mind / UK-based Mental Health Charity
Website: www.mind.org.uk
Telephone Number: 0300 123 3393
Email: info@mind.org.uk
Post: Mind Infoline, PO Box 75225, London E15 9FS

Mind is a fantastic hub of information, with extensive search features and a dedicated team who can point you in the direction of support in your regional area should you be looking for support closer to home.

Nightline Association / University Listening Services
Website: nightline.ac.uk

Students, this one is for you. University can be a challenging environment for any number of reasons. A significant number of universities now have a Nightline service for students; it may be worth seeing if your university is one of them.

The Nightline Association provide an anonymous, confidential, non-judgemental, non-directive listening service. This unique service is run by students, for students.

CALM (Campaign Against Living Miserably)
Website: www.thecalmzone.net
Telephone Number: 0800 58 58 58
Extensive Services Directory
Instant Messaging Service

The Campaign Against Living Miserably (Calm) takes an active approach to standing up against suicide by supporting individuals and campaigning out in society.

Switchboard / LGBT-Specific Helpline
Website: switchboard.lgbt
Telephone Number: 0800 0119 100
Email: hello@switchboard.lgbt
Instant Messaging Service

Switchboard is an LGBT-specific service, where all volunteers are also part of the LGBTQ+ community. They are a safe charity to call upon for emotional well-being support, and one of their primary aspirations is that all individuals in the community will feel 'informed and empowered'.

Mermaids / Support Service for Transgender, Non-Binary and Gender Diverse Individuals
Website: mermaidsuk.org.uk
Telephone Number: 0808 801 0400
Text Chat: 85258
Instant Messaging Service

Mermaids supports transgender, non-binary, and gender-diverse individuals. As one of the UK's leading LGBTQ+ organisations, Mermaids has come alongside thousands of individuals and their families – reducing isolation and improving the awareness and understanding of teachers, medical teams, and social services in addition to other professional bodies.

Cruse Bereavement / UK Bereavement Charity
Website: www.cruse.org.uk
Telephone Number: 0808 808 1677
Register Online for Email Support
80 Local Branches Open Across the UK

Several of these letters drew attention to the experience of grief, which is why I wanted to highlight Cruse Bereavement as somewhere to turn to.

Cruse supports individuals through, what can be, a devastatingly painful process. With 1-2-1 support, community groups, information, and advocacy – Cruse are a reliable charity for grief support.

BEAT / Supporting Those Living With
or Impact By An Eating Disorder
Website: www.beateatingdisorders.org.uk

BEAT is a phenomenal charity, specialising in disordered eating (for those with a diagnosis and those without – with the understanding that *everybody* is deserving of support).

With so many services, information pages, and support groups available on their website, the best thing to do is to head straight there (as each area has unique phone lines and support availability). Beat can support you, and your family, through whatever circumstances you face – 365 days a year!

Samaritans | 'Whatever You're Facing, A Samaritan Will Face It With You'
Website: www.samaritans.org
Telephone Number: 116 123
Email: jo@samaritans.org
Post: Freepost SAMARITANS LETTERS

Samaritans are perhaps the most well-known helpline provider. Supporting individuals, at crisis point or otherwise, Samaritans are there 24 hours a day and 365 days a year for whatever you're facing (what a phenomenal team of volunteers).

Scope | Disability Equality Charity (England & Wales)
Website: www.scope.org.uk
Telephone Number: 0808 800 3333
Email: helpline@scope.org.uk
Textphone Service: Dial 18001 then 0808 800 3333

Scope is England and Wales's disability equality charity – providing emotional support to anybody with a disability and campaigning for a 'fairer society'. Their extensive website is also full of practical information, and volunteers are on hand should you find it helpful to speak with somebody. Scope offers support in a variety of ways – including 1-2-1 sign-interpreted video calls, language-interpreted phone calls, online support, and links in your local area.

Phone Apps To Check Out

Headspace	www.headspace.com
Calm	www.calm.com
Stay Alive	www.stayalive.app
Calm Harm	calmharm.co.uk
Finch	finchcare.com
Iamme	www.iammeapp.com

Books To Read
The Comfort Book by Matt Haig
The Boy, The Mole The Fox and The Horse by Charlie Mackesy
Everything Happens For A Reason and Other Lies I've Loved by Kate Bowler
My Shadow Is Purple by Scott Stuart
All Along You Were Blooming by Morgan Harper Nichols

Of course, it is also worth remembering that you can speak to those around you: friends and family, an individual you trust, a counsellor (do ask for recommendations locally should you think that speaking to somebody professionally would be helpful), or your GP.

Whoever you speak to, I hope they can be all you need them to be in that moment. If not, don't be disheartened – you may not have found the right fit yet. Hold in there, and allow others in.

A percentage of the profits generated by this book will be split between two charities: PAPYRUS and TIC+.

PAPYRUS Prevention of Young Suicide is the UK charity dedicated to the prevention of young suicide. The charity supports individuals under the age of 35 who are experiencing thoughts of suicide, and anyone at any age who is concerned for a young person who may be experiencing thoughts of suicide. Advisors at PAPYRUS can help set up unique safety plans alongside individuals, which can be revisited even after the initial contact has taken place. HOPELINK is a practical and pragmatic way of keeping a safety plan to hand during those hardest moments. PAPYRUS's suicide prevention helpline, HOPELINE247, is also able to support professionals as they work alongside young people, or work through their own experiences – working with first responders, doctors, nurses, police officers, counsellors, teachers, and pastoral staff.

In addition to this, PAPYRUS advocate for change in the community – researching how things are changing, sharing their knowledge far and wide, and speaking up for those impacted by suicide. This book was born out of a need to share a message of hope. Hope parallels the vision of PAPYRUS, so it made sense to me to raise money and awareness for them.

TIC+ is a charity that supports young people living in Gloucestershire, and their families, with free counselling services. While there are many charities that could benefit from support at this time, TIC+ is the charity that provided me with a phenomenal counsellor in a real moment of need. The team's vision is something that I am only too glad to stand behind, and I hope even a small donation will make a difference to the lives of fellow young people.

In purchasing, this book, you are also supporting these two wonderful charities – thank you.